The Royal Guard

Ashley Charles Thwaites

THE ROYAL GUARD

ISBN 978-1-7394079-0-2

Chapter 1
Asylum Born And Bred

I bet I was the only juvenile on planet Earth who didn't need the use of a Ouija board to contact the dead, but not just any dead! I regularly communicated with deceased members of the British Monarchy. Who and how? We will get to that. The Royal Family are more than capable of spreading flammable plots and explosive storylines but, nevertheless, you would be dumb to think they could match me. I am the fuse, BOOM!

At the beginning, my unimaginable story ignited within the walls of an asylum when I was just a child, accepted by staff and inmates, from the age of four, as a polite and inquisitive boy, seemingly fearless even when faced with absolute madness. It was what every child's nightmares were made of. From killer clowns to brain-eating zombies, my childhood night terrors could have never prepared me for that initial spine-chilling asylum welcome that I received.

The building itself gave me an overwhelming eerie feeling, almost as if that anybody who dared to enter such a place would never make it back out alive. On that first exciting day, I dealt with the fear alone in my head instead of expressing the true terror that I was feeling. The new surroundings that I was about to enter would leave me with an indelible impression, imprinted on my being, leaving me feeling as if I was always being followed. Somehow a piece of that asylum was imbedded within my soul from that day even after I had physically left the spine-tingling building.

I was met by the asylum's welcoming party of wild and untamed inhabitants. The sheer volume of manic individuals of all shapes and sizes, with an unlimited amount of facial and body deformities to grab your attention, was overpowering. Their enthusiastic presence, together with their howls and savage screams, made it feel like I was being held captive and the surrounding walls were closing in on me.

My mother, and for that terrifying day my protector, was unable to shield me from all the unconditional attention shown by the unkept patients, so I was forced to hold onto her waist as tightly as my tiny child hands had ever done. I could feel the fear rushing through every cell in my body – which subsequently caused a sudden explosion of all the natural defence senses in my body. I became alert to each individual sound, movement and danger in every direction with an internal radar system searching for every imminent enemy attack.

I immediately realised that these uncontrollable patients had already positioned themselves strategically, ensuring that all the possible exits and my pre-planned escape route – dodging around the blood and other bodily fluids – were blocked, and this only enhanced my feeling of captivity. The fear of the dangers surrounding me made it feel like my heart was beating out of my chest; my hands quivered and my palms became so moist with sweat that I began to lose the tight grip that I had on Mother. Then suddenly, while my attention was on my slippery hands, something got past my body's natural security radar. Out of nowhere, I felt a tight grab and then a tug on my arm and I realised that I was being pulled from Mother's grasp and her secure protection, towards what felt like a hungry pack of meat-eating piranhas at feeding time.

My body froze in terror, and when I tried to scream no noise left my mouth. As I was being pulled away from Mother's safety, I saw that the expression and smile on her face showed no concern or panic; instead she seemed to encourage the patients' excitement for my attention as she released me like a dove taking his first flight into their alternative world of existence. Within seconds it felt like I was being pulled into a black hole at the speed of light. I was being dragged with such force, and without the support of Mother to pull me back to her safety and resist the impact, I had no choice but to stop resisting. As my arm, which only just remained attached to my body at this point, was being pulled towards the face of one of my captors, I prepared myself mentally to be eaten alive right there on the spot.

I closed my eyes and tensed my whole body in terrifying anticipation, to only then be physically and emotionally mauled as they pulled intensely at my heartstrings while sniffing, kissing, nibbling, and even licking any of my skin that was visible and accessible to them. It was the most unusual behaviour I had ever witnessed, as if they had the mentality of a pack of wolves, being the judge and jury for my acceptance into their wolf pack. I froze like a statue, as if I had momentarily stopped breathing to allow their physical, but voiceless, interrogation of me.

I wasn't sure who the alpha was in the room, so I didn't dare stare anyone in the eyes for too long as I did not want to appear to be a threat to anybody. Instead I stood there terrified among their moans and growls, with my tail tucked between my legs. I just allowed them to gather their information from my overactive sweat glands under my unsevered arms. I quickly learnt that the aggressive affection shown to me by the patients was anything but aggression; instead I was educated about an uncontrollable, unfairly not tolerated, and unconditional love. That day it felt like I was being taught to swim among the sharks of the asylum by being thrown into the deep end. Most people would have run and never looked back, or hoped this was all just a nightmare. Not me, as when I should have been terrified, I instead found comfort in the asylum and its residents.

As a family we were very animal orientated and always had at least a couple of goats as pets, as well as a whole host of other animals. We would keep the goats on ropes by their shed in our back garden, which would give them access to more grazing. Mum would tell us we had them just so my dad did not have to mow the lawns, but I knew there was more to it than that. Just like dogs, they needed exercising and we would walk them through the fields to the asylum to safely deliver or collect Mother from work. The patients whom they came into contact with would have had differences of opinions when it came to petting them, as for some I was introducing them to the first goat they had ever seen.

I remember one of the most amusing of times when my father allowed our pet goat into a ward where Mother was working – a ward which had its own doorway into the courtyard. The ward had a separate sitting room where patients would congregate during the day. To enable some patients who were physically unable to get out into the courtyard to see the goat, Mum allowed the goat into this room, only to have a patient open the separating door, which enabled the goat to get into the main ward where all the other patients were.

I can remember both screaming and laughing patients.

From then onwards, goats were officially banned from the ward by Mother. We had a dog who also enjoyed the walk and during the light summer months, we would always take full advantage of the beautiful asylum grounds.

My constant presence at the asylum became invisible to the staff as they struggled to cope with under-staffing at the institution. It was as if I had turned into a chameleon or was wearing camouflage; I became the invisible boy who sat and listened, unnoticed, as they had conversations about the patients. The best source of information was when I overheard the gossip during the regular hand-over between shifts, during which the staff would pass on the entire day's juicy facts to the next shift.

When I didn't witness it with my own eyes, the staff would use incidents involving patients and their strange behaviour to entertain me; sometimes this even went as far as re-enacting the incidents as they took out their frustrations that were otherwise cleverly silenced by the powers and resources above their pay scale. People forget that a child's mind acts as a dry sponge that, when thrown into a bucket of water, soaks up everything around it. When I was four years old my brain was more than twice as active as any of the adults around me at the asylum; this continued until the age of ten. From the age of four my ideas and beliefs were being moulded by what I had witnessed and heard around me, and would go on to change my life.

These lapses by the staff came despite the strict confidentiality agreements that they signed, and even as they let slip the secrets of their charges, they would whisper, 'What happens in the asylum, stays in the asylum.' To the young child born within a stone's throw from the asylum walls in September 1977, life served up strange and disturbing knowledge that I was not yet old enough to process.

My norm was insanity.

The threat of losing their jobs, and a very impressive pension plan, kept the secrets hidden. I was learning valuable lessons that would remain with me forever, just as any child would be a victim of their upbringing. However, I carried more than an ordinary child on my young shoulders, for from that very age I knew of a conspiracy that could rock the nation – a royal conspiracy.

Members of the Royal Family were being killed all around me, literally. Worse still, my connection to the place meant that I became a part of it.

Who would have imagined that a child born less than a mile away from an asylum would have a quantum entanglement with one of our monarchy's biggest and darkest secrets, a secret which would alter a country's history and leave at least six members of our Royal Family dead and forgotten?

How can a monarchy have the authority to kill their own, issuing cold and calculated punishment against family members? How unjust could life be to have been brought into this world as a member of one of the wealthiest and most powerful families in the world, only for those powers to then be used against them?

These powers being used against individuals to be lawfully killed would be bad enough, but to have their lives erased from the nation's history books is surely an injustice to the nation and the world. How could people kill their own family, while others accept and allow it to happen?

The simple fact was that they were dead because they were different and had imperfections. There is nothing gracious in the Royal Family's ignorance and neglect of their own; there is nothing noble about lies and deceit. We have no choice but to live with a monarchy of unelected forces that still wields great power, while we pay for their lavish existence with millions of tax pounds each year.

When the interests of the family 'firm' become more important than that of the individual member, is that not fascism at work? Should all activities be allowed, and to go unanswered? They carry out their dance of power while we are only given the information we are allowed and supposed to know. Our perception of our Royal Family comes through the images and stories they allow to be featured in our media, the media which is partially controlled by those very royals and their entourages.

I have seen with my own eyes the hive of lies and villainy, and the outcome of what our British establishment will do to keep its reputation. It would be hard to believe what I have witnessed in my lifetime, even I struggled to accept the wilful ignorance of what they have done. There was never an apology for what happened to these six members of our Royal Family. Did anyone lift a finger to correct the record? Never.

Even as a child, I realised that the world around the royals was changing, but all they seemed to care about was self-preservation. Their actions were the beginning of the events that laid the foundations for my life's decisions and its meaning. They always had a choice; at the end of the day they are the Royal Family. It felt as if they had made the wrong decisions, leaving me with only one.

There was always going to be a strong connection between me and the asylum; after all, the room in which I first entered the world had a clear and daunting view of the three magnificent towers that rose above the ancient building that housed the asylum. Mother told me that when the asylum siren sounded, which was very regularly, Father would turn off the mobile in my cot, because the rising and falling sound of the siren, similar to those heard during air raids in the wars, would seem to pacify and comfort me more than the nursery rhymes played from my mobile. Even while being fed at my mother's breast, I would stop feeding to hear the loud and distinctive siren seemingly beckoning me towards the asylum.

Four years after my birth, when I no longer required the constant care and watchful eye that an infant does, my mother decided she would seek new employment. Living so close to the asylum and being a kind, naturing and compassionate person, she decided she would like to work there. She got a job as a nursing assistant caring for the patients within, very quickly became fond of the residents, and enjoyed, even loved, the work and connections she was making with the individuals who lived there. I was very proud of the work she was doing and the new role she played in the patients' lives. She would always go the extra mile just as she did at home, and she was very motherly to the patients, treating them with dignity and showing respect at all times.

Being the youngest and newest edition to the family, my mother loved to show me off. I was introduced to her work friends and many of the asylum's patients. Once she went back to work she missed the time we had spent together, and thus a mother's attachment to her child was the catalyst for events that would rock a nation.

Those first four years of my life were special to us both, and we formed an unbreakable bond. As much as she loved her new job, Mother missed her baby boy, so would grasp every extra minute with me. As she became more comfortable within her position at the asylum, helped by the relaxed atmosphere created by the other staff, she began to introduce me to even more of their world and the inhabitants within the walls of the institution.

Unaware of what I would later uncover, I got to know all the patients my mother looked after, as well as many of the others from around the asylum. After some initial nervousness, something any child would have when meeting somebody new, even outside of an asylum, I began to love these forgotten souls – accepting and treating them as if they were my extended family. I felt a powerful reciprocation of love, and unconditional bonds were forged. Over time, my existence at the asylum became increasingly accepted and was never questioned. I was either welcomed or just ignored. There was nobody watching the creepy grounds or corridors, and no guards or cameras for the patients' safety or mine. I was able to wander as freely as the patients. Very quickly, I felt comfortable within the dark and unnerving surroundings of the asylum.

The only things that seemed royal about the Royal Earlswood Asylum were the grounds and entrance hall, both of which were on show to the public. Being lavish and elegant created an illusion, masking and disguising a very different place to the one containing the horrors and mystery that have been etched into my memory. Royal Earlswood was situated among four acres of stunningly well-kept lawns that were abundant with wildlife. There were the regular appearances of foxes, rabbits and squirrels. On many occasions, I even saw badgers and deer. Even outside you were unable to get away from the sense of the history the building held – it stood out as one of a kind compared with any other building in its proximity, with a faint hint of haunted mansions or vampire castles so beloved of creepy movies.

When Mother was not taking on extra duties during the day, she would work regular night shifts. Three nights on followed by four nights off, then vice versa. Father and I would take her to and from the asylum, walking through the grounds greeting and meeting patients, and often enjoying a cup of tea with the residents on the wards while waiting for Mother.

The asylum had a huge, well-kept, swooping drive, with far too many unnecessary curves and bends, adding to the austerity of the external view. We often used an entrance through the field opposite our house to get there as it was the most direct route, but Mother regularly complained about having to walk through long grass and brambles. Facing the front of the building were two parallel lines of the tallest oak trees I had ever seen.

They were tall and wide, as if reaching up into the clouds, and I remember thinking that they were rounder than the paddling pool we had at home, which my childish eye thought was huge. From the gnarled appearance of their trunks they looked like they had been there for hundreds of years. In complete contrast to the interior of the building, the skin of the exterior stood astonishingly elegant. The huge Victorian windows resembled those on the Royal homes in London, only thirty minutes away from the asylum. Just walking onto the grounds and having the picturesque building in view made me feel as if I were stepping back into Victorian times – especially on a foggy morning when the land was alive with the wildlife.

The grounds were very peaceful and quiet – that is except for the screams, which could not be contained within the sound-proofed building. If you got there at just the right time, when shifts had changed and patients were being counted, there was no-one around the outside of the building, leaving you in a tranquil and private place where your imagination could run wild.

On entering the building through the main entrance, there was a beautiful hallway leading to a cold, stone staircase that took you up to the headquarters of the operation. Just off from the entrance hall there was a stunning conference room containing an oversized, solid oak table. There was always a man sitting at a desk at the far end of the hall, under the semi-spiral staircase, constantly managing the old-fashioned, internal phone system. I would watch him as he pulled the pins that held the phone lines, transferring calls to the correct wards. Usually after just one word or two, he would move the connection point from one hole into another. The large board with all the different connections and dials resembled the inside of a spaceship.

An immaculate, bright red carpet, running the length of the front hall and up the staircase, stood out against the plain stone floors and walls. At the top of the first set of steps stood a giant golden bust, really rounding off the illusion that this place was something it actually was not. The offices that housed the important staff were far away from the patients, behind heavy and difficult to open doors.

I found that the heaviest and most difficult doors to open in the whole asylum were at the back of this entrance hall. Having been on the other side of these partitions, I knew exactly how firm and heavy they were. I had regularly seen, and heard, patients banging their heads hard against them, wanting to pass through or just to express their distress. You did not need to enter or open these doors to hear the constant screams and yelling, which echoed down the asylum corridors – but enter and you were in another world entirely.

One or two of these tortured souls would be allowed beyond their world, to sit and watch our world on chairs in the grand reception. It was these more able residents who would come to me as soon as I entered, craving affection and looking to assist or direct me around the asylum. You could tell instantly that they were patients by their badly fitted and scruffy clothing, usually complete with stains from their last meal. Along with this crew, there was also a man who was regularly found rocking in a chair at the far right corner of the hall, with a bag full to the brim with magazines. Not a specific one that he followed, just masses of any variety he could get his hands on. They would be so crammed into his plastic carrier bag that most of the pages were torn or creased. He would sit there flicking through one of his magazines looking at all the pictures. He would look at them so closely that his head would touch the page. It was unimaginable he could even see the illustrations with his eyes so close, but when questioned on his reading material he would always have the correct answers.

The entrance hall was one of the many charades and scams of the asylum, leaving you with the impression that you were somewhere you really were not. It was never clear to me if the heavy doors were there to keep the less able patients contained or to keep hidden the secrets and lies that were held within.

From a very young age, while others were learning their multiplications or how to ride a bike, I was being trained in the art of deceit. I was taught to lie for what those around me supposed was the greater good. This was in the beginning before I realised the greater good was neither greater nor good. This was before I had my part to play and my own greater good became a necessity and obsession.

The royal secrets were not the only ones behind those doors; there were also the asylum's secrets and procedures. Things I witnessed growing up would alter my life. Behind those doors, without regret or concern, human rights seemed to be forgotten. Nearly all these patients had a life without love or the support of a family. The staff became their carers, family, friends and, in some cases, worst enemies. Abuse was abundant and widely accepted, and inside the asylum walls there existed a deeper and darker world than you could ever imagine. Many of the patients, I later learned, came from the very top of society, and yet they were hidden in the shadows where they caused no one any embarrassment: dirty little secrets that had been covered up by the people who ran the asylum and appreciated the lavish endowments they got from the families, their most influential donors.

Every human being's genetic make-up tells us whether or not he or she possesses the 'kindness gene,' An individual's genotype shows us that those carrying two copies of the G gene have the ability to behave in a way that benefits other people, and in contrast those with the A version genotype have lower levels of these positive emotions – empathy, and compassion. It is surprising how many individuals lacking the 'kindness gene' take on careers within the care industry. I believe we create our own demons, and I'm sure that some of the doctors and staff are haunted by their actions within the asylum walls.

I do not believe that all of the asylum abusers started off that way, but that much of their behaviour develops at the asylum. I would watch the staff's behaviour become as institutionalised as the patients' habits. Others simply became sheep and would copy the behaviour of other staff without conscience. It would seem that people were intentionally blind to the abuse that was everywhere. The abusers weren't hidden or disguised; they walked proudly among their colleagues. I was witness to daily examples of people with power using that power to manipulate vulnerable people in their trust.

If only people had known what was happening behind those closed doors, or if only those who were aware had changed things from within, my life would have been very different. The abuse and terror I was to witness seemed endless but was never spoken of; the staff lived in their own world with their own set of rules. Even I did not know, or understand, the full extent of what I was witness to until many years after the offences had happened. It was my hidden kingdom. The patients were both institutionalised and medicated to keep them unaware of the world beyond the grounds; without knowing anything different they even seemed happy to accept what they were going through.

I grew up on the story of our historical battles, the Crown and its honour. In the films I watched on television, good people were always portrayed as fighting for what was right, and we were fooled into believing that our Royal family does not do things that are wrong to get the results they think are right, whatever the consequences. If you were to believe that for all of us life is about correcting our mistakes, then you would be deluded.

I shared my childhood with these people, the hidden insane. The asylum became my kingdom and wonderland, and the grounds became an extension to my garden. The thought of spending your childhood in a creepy asylum might not sound appealing to most, but to me it was both dangerous and exciting; in fact it was in many ways all that a little boy with adventure on his mind could ever ask for.

I would soon learn the dark stories that resided within these walls, secrets that would dominate my life, leaving me questioning the truth at every turn. Could this be the place where I would be taught that the love for power is stronger than the power of love? Could the secrets of the Royal deaths be buried here? From the highest order of our society, I would hold information that could bring people back from the dead, or even put them there.

Chapter 2
Breakfast Terrors

Honk, it sounded, and honk again, in response to the piercing noise imparting the chilling knowledge that there was trouble at the asylum.

Honk, honk. Drowned under the siren call to action.

Honk, honk it went again, and my finely-tuned ear detected that my brass horn had a dent in it; more than one dent – in fact one for every previous adventure.

'Ashley, stop doing that, that's enough now,' came my father's voice. He was always a hater of any of my imaginary games that included loud noises or his participation.

'Dad, we have another escaped patient,' I'd replied. 'I'm letting them know I had no sightings, it's important.'

It was important to me, excitingly important. However, to my parents it was the cost of living within a stone's throw of the asylum. Good for Mother, when her child slowed down her usual rush to be away from domestic bliss and towards being ankle deep in insanity. Good for Father, me and the family dog, Snoopy, because we could walk him across the field in just minutes and pop in to see her at any time. For

Father, the almost daily siren was yet another intrusion of my mother's work into his life; for me it was a call to arms.

Honk, honk, honk, my horn would bellow back over the sound of the siren as I sat inside my watchtower and observed the asylum through the trees. My father had crafted it out of old timber, in the tallest weeping willow in our garden. I had a clear view of the yellow- and red-brick tower at the Royal Earlswood Asylum and was in excellent earshot of the regular siren that could be heard for miles. It heralded something deeply exciting, and it was quite disappointing when I found out, as a teenager, that the alarm was tested regularly and those screeching sirens were no more than a test, not the screams of escaping madmen. However, at the time, it added to the excitement and danger I lusted after in life. Hearing the call from the luxury of my home was a constant reminder of the asylum's existence, and was soon to become a continuous reminder of my duties within the walls – a subliminal message.

In those early days, we would take Snoopy with us to the asylum. He was a real favourite with the patients. If I knew then what I would grow up to learn, I would have never taken any of our beloved family pets into the grounds. However, I didn't know and the trip across the field to meet Mother often included a pet or two. I loved the times when we would take our pet goat for a walk through the asylum grounds and even inside some of the wards to see the less-mobile patients. I do not think they had ever seen a goat before, and when one of the goats broke free of my grasp and ate all the plants it was priceless. Even though the goat chased several of the patients around the ward, they all seemed to be highly amused once it was recaptured. The staff were very relaxed about the frequent visits by assorted animals, and the patients found it very exciting. Even at that age – I was about eight – I really enjoyed, and was intrigued with, sharing new experiences and introducing the patients to new activities, however strange.

One of my best memories is that every Saturday morning my father would take me into town and buy me a new toy – there were only a few toyshops in town so the choice was not great, but to me these were magical places where I had Father's undivided attention.

Every Sunday, after church, we would go to the asylum as a family and I would take whatever new toy I had bought the day before to show the patients. I loved the look of excitement and amazement on their faces as they shared in the enjoyment of my new purchase. We would have a roast dinner in the staff canteen and then spend time with various patients on the wards. It might sound strange for a child, but this was a treat for me as I loved any extra visits there. While my parents drank cups of tea with the staff, I would interact and play games with the patients. I was brought up to believe we were all part of one giant family and we should love, respect and take care of each other in the best ways we could. Mother cared and protected the patients as if they were her own children, and many of my fondest family memories were at the asylum. The majority of the patients had no family or connection to anyone in the outside world, so we were really their family.

Not all of our relatives and friends understood Mother's devotion to her work and her patients, and I remember one dinner party when things did not go so well.

Mother had been feeling a bit guilty for spending so much time at the asylum and neglecting Father, so she decided to throw a grand party for his friends. Well, their friends, as Father rarely did anything on his own and preferred the comfort of family to a night out with the boys.

However, Mother was determined that he would have fun

and as the evening approached she was busier than ever, treating her patients by night and preparing the house for the party by day.

'Would you like to invite one of your friends, darling,' she asked me a few days before the dinner was due.

I thought for a while, and then came upon the person I most liked to be with. 'Yes, Catherine.'

'I don't know a Catherine, darling, is she a school friend?' Mother asked.

'No, not school, Mummy. You know her, that lady with the big scar on her throat. I know she is a bit smelly, but we could clean her up and give her one of your nice dresses,' I explained.

'What are you talking about?'

'You know her, all the nurses bow in front of her and everyone laughs. She must be very important.'

'The nurses? Do you mean someone from the asylum?' Mother said, looking really shocked.

'Uh ha,' I affirmed, suddenly feeling less sure about my choice.

'Oh, you are so lovely, but we can't invite patients to our home.'

'Why?'

'Just because,' Mother said in her this-is-the-end-of-the-subject voice.

'B... but,' I stammered, rather shocked at her attitude.

'Darling, they are not our friends, and they are locked up for a reason. If you are getting attached to the patients I will have to stop you visiting, darling, it's not healthy.'

I held my opinion of this attitude deep inside for fear of a volcanic eruption. How could my mother, the woman who treated those lovely people, not feel they were family?

On the night, although I was so young, I was allowed to

stay up and meet the guests. My parents never really got that their children were children. We were treated as adults most of the time. I guess that if they had thought of us as children who needed to be shielded they would never have exposed us to the insane. All in all, I am glad my parents were so unaware of how inappropriate some might find our way of life. My parents were professionals by trade, but in many ways they were quite bohemian.

I was sitting on a poof next to the fire, cuddled up to Mother and creasing up her new taffeta dinner gown, when one of my father's friends almost made a fatal mistake.

'So when are you going to join the compos mentis world?' he asked, thinking he was being rather funny.

I felt Mother's hand go to the fire poker and then think better of it. Perhaps the inmates were rubbing off on her a little, I thought.

'Is that a dig at my patients?' she asked with a charming smile as sharp as a knife in the back.

'Well, you are working with the insane,' he smirked and then immediately caught himself,

'And we all applaud you, of course we do. But working in an asylum, really? Is that where your skills are best employed?'

'And where would you have me employ my skills?' Mother asked, the smile still poised to reveal teeth that could tear out his throat.

'There are lots of private patients who would pay a fortune for your help. Real people with problems you can help them face,' he said, and even to me, a mere child, he sounded snobbish.

'I'm sorry my patients don't live up to your high standards, but believe it or not they are human beings that need help every bit as much as anyone else. They are patients and not criminals and deserve the care that everyone else gets. They are no bearded ladies or elephant men to be gawked at as if they were some mutation worthy only of the fair ground,' Mother said, her voice dripping with contempt.

'They are from some of the best families,' I added, just to be shushed by my father who, despite having turned rather red, was smiling in approval at his strong wife.

I have to admit, by the time I was sent up to bed I felt sorry for the man; he could not stop apologising profusely. My mother had shown her grit and I was happy that she did see the patients as people, just like me. She would come to call them friends, I was sure.

No matter how much Mother might defend the asylum, no one who spent time there, even someone of my tender years, could fail to notice a difference and a lack of continuity in the level of care given by the different members of staff – not only seen by looking at the patients' appearance, their level of cleanliness, and personal hygiene, but in the tone and manner in which these individuals were being spoken to. Some staff would bark orders, while others would be gentle and ask nicely. The good carers stuck out like a sore thumb; they seemed to love what they were doing and had a sense of achievement in helping somebody. They had an aura about them, happy and smiling, with an actual sensitive touch. They never rushed or lost their patience with the residents.

Some of the staff would come to work with their own agenda and way of running their shift, preferring to get all the necessary physical work over and done with efficiently at the beginning of their shift, even if it meant doing so at irregular and unnatural times, rather than keeping to the patient's regular routine. This would unsettle and disorientate many of the patients and make them more agitated and so more difficult to handle. One day I witnessed this first hand as I observed the patients' institutionalised and monotonous routine. I was sitting quietly, almost hidden, on a ward where there was a calm and peaceful atmosphere – that is, until Leanne cut through it like a combine harvester ploughing through a crisp field of ripe corn. Leanne was in serious work mode and had her own schedule for the work she wished to get out of the way. I looked up from the comic I was reading to the sound of Leanne insisting on Richard having his bath 'immediately'. Richard was nice and cosy in an armchair watching television as if it was his whole world.

Richard ignored the first command from Leanne, which seemed to ignite a spark inside her. Leanne stomped across the room to confront Richard, standing over him and glaring down at him with a burning stare that could have melted solid stone, but he still sat comfortably snuggled in his armchair. The next time Leanne opened her mouth, the voice that erupted from the toxic hole was much louder, with a tone that was terrifying and extremely threatening. Even I froze in fear for him. It was so quiet you could have heard a raindrop in the courtyard, but on the inside I was yelling to Richard to comply quickly.

It was with all this commotion that thankfully, like an angel from heaven, Lucy came from the other side of the ward to intervene and save Richard from the anticipated attack. Lucy was a young and attractive girl but was disliked by the other members of staff as she always had a kinder way of doing things; she also had her own opinions and a voice that she was not afraid to use. She went against the grain and the usual standards set by the asylum's staff. Lucy could see that Leanne was agitated and short-fused. I think the whole room noticed it as they watched, stunned frozen in terror as their fellow housemate was victimised by Leanne.

'What's the commotion?' Lucy asked.

'It's nothing I can't handle,' Leanne barked.

'Obviously you can't, you can cut the atmosphere with a

knife,' Lucy said, putting a reassuring hand on Richard's shoulder.

'Look, he needs to have his bath now, but he won't budge. We are not their servants, I can't stand around till his lordship is ready. It's bath time and that's that. I have to get on with running the ward and the shift will not go smoothly if he does not obey,' Leanne ranted, throwing Richard a threatening look.

This wasn't Lucy's first rodeo with Leanne, just a re-run of a previous episode. Lucy was fully aware of Leanne's overzealous and escalating aggressive approach, and the consequences that would follow. Before Lucy had time to block Leanne's predictable next move, the first assault and unorthodox grapple was unleashed on Richard. Without any verbal warning, Leanne grabbed at Richard's shoulder and pulled him from his chair. Defending himself, Richard pushed her away from him while groaning an unmistakable 'no'. He was clearly wound up by this physical attack and pushed away all the subsequent aggressive advances from Leanne.

This was when Lucy made her move. It was very brave of Lucy and quite a rare occurrence within the asylum, as even I knew the repercussions for her working relationship not only with Leanne, but also with the hidden cell of institutionalised staff who lived by strict rules similar to those of a secret society.

'Leanne, please, he didn't do anything. It's his favourite television programme and it really isn't his bath time yet. Just calm down, you are terrifying everyone,' Lucy pleaded, trying to defuse the situation and stop it from escalating any further. 'Please stop winding him up, let's have a happy shift today.'

'You let these freaks get away with too much. Just go back to your side of the ward and stop sticking your nose into other people's business,' Leanne growled, holding on firmly to the now snivelling Richard. 'I have to bath his lordship now so we can have a peaceful shift,' she continued, and it flashed across my mind that she was putting a great deal of emphasis on the words 'his lordship'. Was this another example of the cruelty of our ruling classes?

'I just want a nice, peaceful shift, understand?' Leanne blared at Richard. It was anything but peacefulness; Leanne was creating all the commotion.

'I am sorry, but he is not going anywhere, Leanne,' Lucy said, getting between the two opponents.

Richard whimpered as he was freed from Leanne's clutches, falling to the floor in a ball.

Lucy knelt down next to Richard, looked him in the eyes, and calmly asked him if he would come and have a bath. I wasn't sure if Richard's immediate and definite refusal to the soft and gentle request by Lucy was due to his interest in the television programme or Leanne's threatening commands and physical assault. Lucy begged Richard once again to go with her, only to receive a firm 'No' accompanied by a negative hand gesture. I could see Leanne's frustration levels rising with the hold-up to her schedule and plans for a relaxed shift. Lucy could see the annoyance on Leanne's face and the hostility in her body language, so she quickly stood back up and again pleaded with Leanne on Richard's behalf, showing a rare diversity in the care she, as an individual, provided by changing her approach to meet the patient's needs. Leanne was treating Richard the same way that I once treated a hamster that bit the end of my finger, and was thereafter kept in his cage only to be fed, watered, and occasionally cleaned.

'Look, he won't be any more trouble, let him just watch a bit more TV and he will go willingly wherever you want, I'll make sure of it. There won't be any more trouble, just back away for a little and the shift will be smooth and peaceful,' Lucy promised Leanne. It was like watching someone bribe a child into a van with sweets. I think she would have told her anything to get the desired answer and defuse the situation for poor Richard.

I could see that Leanne was not happy but she was left with few options as Lucy was not going to stand down.

'OK, but on your head be it,' warned Leanne before she walked away disgruntled, muttering profanities under her breath. It was such a relief as slowly the room regained the calmness it had before this storm blew in. Their world was once again at peace; well, all except for the whispering and sniggering coming from the side room, where Leanne could be heard complaining and name-smearing Lucy to the other staff. I could see them watching Lucy as they mocked her rebellious attitude. You would have thought that she had sworn at the Pope. Even a child could see that they were completely wrong and misguided. I saw the incident with my own eyes. Through their smeared optic lenses they had been convinced by Leanne that Lucy was no longer a team player, and had thus been branded an enemy and tarnished with the plague.

A very short while later, I saw Leanne watch Lucy leave the lounge area to carry out her other duties. Lucy had unknowingly left Richard without her protection for less than two minutes, and I could already see Leanne eying up her prey as would a blood-thirsty wild panther. Without any warning and regard for the previous incident or the conversation with Lucy, Leanne pounced, marched directly to Richard's chair and proceeded to raise the back, trying to lift Richard from his seated position. Richard was very startled by this physical attack as he did not see his predator approaching, once again absorbed in the television. Richard held onto the chair tightly, causing Leanne to manoeuvre herself from the back of the chair to the front, where Richard would be forced to confront his raging aggressor face to face.

'You are coming with me, Richard?' Leanne snapped at him with a terrifying voice as she grabbed him once again, but this time with much more force than she had during the previous incident.

Richard was resisting and groaning the word 'No' to her, but this time in reply Leanne deliberately stamped on Richard's feet, causing him instant discomfort and unnecessary physical and emotional botheration. The pain she inflicted caused him to be momentarily distracted and to lose his concentration and grip of the chair's arms. With the speed of a snapping turtle, she grabbed Richard's legs by his trousers and pulled him from his chair down to the floor with a loud thud. It was so quick that no one in the room seemed to notice anything happening until they heard the loud thud. Except for me, but I remained a silent witness to the whole event. The inhumane behaviour seemed so natural to Leanne, and Richard's groaning and pointless resilience continued as she proceeded to pull Richard across the cold, stone floor by his trousers. Leanne looked pleased with the short-term punishment she had inflicted as well as the long-term lesson and reminder to Richard to not defy her again. Leanne continued to drag Richard across the floor of the asylum until he was out of sight and his groans for help were far in the distance. That was the last I saw of Richard.

I never quite forgot Richard, but I was a child and resilient. My childhood days were among the happiest of my life, but as the years passed, I began to change and become more aware of what went on around me. In those early years I still had no idea that the secrets I was soon to uncover would change my life. One might argue that my parents should never have allowed an infant like me to spend so much time at the asylum.

You might think that all those years as a small child

playing in an asylum full of psychiatric patients could have been a little dangerous and scary; well, it was both at times. I was given safety guidelines by my parents to 'run', 'raise voice', 'get behind a closed door' – which my mother would repeatedly tell me. They were considered to be the three rules I needed to escape any incidents. Mother had taught me to feel safe in the asylum most of the time, and I knew if I was ever in trouble I had to raise my voice, being firm and assertive. I was not to show fear if in trouble, or if I was somehow manhandled by a patient. At times it seemed they would thrive on my every weakness, and they found comfort in my discomfort. It was as if they could smell me out, and were both attracted to and received messages from the fear pheromones I was releasing.

I was born into this danger from the day I could walk, so I had my wits about me at all times. I would enjoy interacting and playing with patients outside the main building, as this provided me with escape routes if I needed them. Inside the asylum I was more restricted and had narrow corridors, walls, or heavy hospital fire doors impeding my escape if I needed to get out of danger.

What was to unfold would soon lead to a small child possibly being to blame, through his innocent actions, for bringing the truth about the Royal deaths crashing down around him. I was a child, but because of me newspapers throughout the world had a story that brought shame to all involved. A story that changed our Royal family's line of succession and the history books forever. Who was to know that I was going to be the reason that the past would catch up and be corrected?

However, I get ahead of myself; that was still to come.

Growing up I did not see many of the dangerous and known to be violent patients, as they were kept locked up, with their own caged-off gardens, like animals in a zoo. From these wards I often heard screams and howling. Wards where every door had a lock on it. It was this confinement in a small, defined area that caused the great distress that produced the haunting screams and uncontrollable banging on walls, rather than the patients' mental illnesses. I would go and watch them through the entrapment; I could see first-hand the anger and distress as they would lash out at each other behind the caged walls. When outside these cages and their locked units, they were herded like cattle from place to place, with the staff leading and securing the rear like you would with convicts. All that seemed to be missing was electric cattle rods.

I was told that these patients were caged for the safety of others and that I was never ever to go anywhere near them. I had no idea what the future had in store for me, or that day I would have run and never seen the asylum again. As I watched these poor souls in my innocence, I would have caught glimpses of the lion who I would one day meet while trapped, without means of escape, in my own caged attack.

As a child looking at these poor souls, my mind went to zombie films – the ones my parents never stopped me from watching, despite their horrific nature. Sometimes it would just seem like the asylum grounds were alive with the walking dead, moving awkwardly in formation and slowly in groups. It wasn't scary as the grounds were so vast and the patients so slow, but occasionally they would head straight towards you, as if there were a homing signal attached to you. Much of the time they wanted nothing more than affection, a kind touch, and playful attention. It was frightening to observe the staff holding on tightly to the backs of the patients' clothing to control and restrict their movement, preventing them from physically attacking and harming one another. If the patient tried to move away they would be strangled by their own clothing and would soon be returned to the deadly march.

I was always made aware of the dangers and risks of the asylum, and I had seen enough incidents myself to scare me and convince me of the risks. Every time I walked the corridors, no matter how many times I had done it previously, my fears were heightened – especially during the evenings. The corridors were long and seemed very narrow, and it was a long way from one area to another, but it was the blood that fascinated me. Every crack and scrape in the white walls seemed to tell a story. One of the only times I would truly feel uneasy was watching the patients run their fingers over these cracks as they walked up and down the corridors. It was as if they became a collective, the patients in front of me somehow connected to the collective of those who had passed those blood-stained corridors for generations. Then there were the times that patients were left lying or sitting on the cold floor, banging their arms and heads against shut doors. That would be quite frightening for anyone, let alone a child.

Heavy doors opened onto these corridors, and even in the dark, I could tell how opened or closed they were by listening carefully for their very distinctive creak. When left to roam these corridors, the patients were usually covered in blood and urine, and I would have to dodge their touch as I passed them. When leaving a ward, I would check first by scanning and listening for doors opening, or any patients being around that I did not know or feel comfortable with. I would then set off walking down the corridors, but would run if I heard one of the large fire doors creaking open or slamming shut. I would always gasp with relief as I escaped the artificially lit corridors to enter a more populated or well-lit area. Whenever my route was blocked, I would run from the darkness and find safety behind other heavy doors, as I knew that I could hold most patients back by pushing against their feeble force.

Mostly I was controlled within the asylum walls by my parents, in an unconventional but very effective way; my mother would tell me ghost and horror stories of the asylum each morning over the breakfast table. It would seem to me that on most shifts there would have been at least one event to keep me entertained over my cereal before school. Each incident would open my eyes to a world that was far more exciting than my own or anything I could possibly have imagined. The stories of deaths, ghosts and full-moon madness were just a small part of what actually went on.

One of the areas I did not like to go into was Cockroach Alley. Mother had told me about one night when she had gone into a dark room where there was an unusual sound with every footstep she took. When she turned on the lights the floor began to move like a conveyor belt. It was alive with cockroaches and the noise she had heard was her feet crushing their armoured, shelled backs. Tales of patients' deaths during the nights while they were sleeping kept me away from the mortuary building, and the stories of madness during full moons meant that I was especially alert when I was on the grounds and within the walls. Growing up in the eighties, vampires and werewolves were all over the TV and in films, so stories of how the 'lunatics', as they were often known outside our home, came alive with the full moon excited and scared me in equal measure.

Mother would tell me how the patients appeared to be more alert and that there seemed to be a release of their tensions at the asylum on the nights of the full moon. She would be so aware of the position of the moon that she would mark it on our kitchen calendar and grow tense when she had to work on her own at the asylum during these energetic and frightening evenings. I imagine that caring for a ward of thirty patients in an asylum alone without support was daunting enough, but with the anticipation of trouble it must have been extremely scary. Especially so as she was a petite woman, alone and all too aware that throughout the world there were reports of heightened crime rates, more frequent traffic accidents, suicides, crisis call-centre calls, dog bites, psychiatric admissions and murders during full moons. I had to see it with my own eyes; I could not believe that the moon could hold such magical powers over the patients at the asylum and held this mystical influence over their behaviour. I considered the full moon as a glorious occasion to admire, but little did I know it was actually when, by using the backdrop of the sparkling sky with brilliant stars, the puppet master came out to manipulate its puppets.

Had the full moon been deceiving me all this time as I had been gazing in awe and amazement of its wonder? Had the moonlight been deceptive, tricking me by its splendour when really it ran havoc and caused mischief within the asylum walls? I needed answers to these questions if only to satisfy my inquisitive nature, as these unbelievable and mind-blowing facts were not being taught to my satisfaction at my school.

One morning over my cornflakes I pleaded with my mother to take me to the asylum on a spooky, full-moon night. She was very reluctant to allow me there on such an unpredictable evening, so like a true professional I immediately put the pressure on by pleading my case and literally begging her. This continued every morning at breakfast until after two painful weeks she finally grew tired of my whining and gave in. I immediately ran to the calendar hanging on the side of the fridge and looked for the moon marking she drew on each month, and put my name against a night during the full moon as a reminder of our verbal – but legally binding – mother and son contract that she was now bound to. I was both excited and nervous to finally either put this myth to rest or face the puppetmaster myself on the frightening and threateningly inauspicious night when he appeared to send unexplainable terrors through the asylum.

When the night of the full moon finally arrived I showed no reluctance as I knew that Mother was looking for any excuse not to take me, but inside my stomach was doing turns like a tumble dryer to match the ominous feeling in the night's chilling air. I wanted to get to the asylum early and before the sun set so I could recognise any changes that happened when the power of the full moon took full effect during the twilight hours. With this in mind, my mother and I went to the asylum earlier than she usually would have for her shift, and instead of going to her home for the night we walked around several wards meeting and greeting a multitude of patients and the minimal staff presence. We sat in numerous wards where my mother drank tea and chatted with the staff while I positioned myself by the windows in nervous anticipation of the sunset, to wait for the unknown terrors to begin. I watched the sun disappear behind the treeline and ran out of the ward to find another window in which I could face the glare of the powerful full moon. The ghostly silver orb expressed beams of moonlight which lasered across the horizon like glittery fire, casting shapes that refused to be defined.

It was hypnotising to watch. I sat there wondering if the moon had already begun to cast its spell over the asylum. I waited by that window for about fifteen minutes and nothing happened. To say that I was disappointed would be an understatement. I left the window seat and moped my way back to join Mother on the ward to explain my disappointment to her.

As I was communicating my sadness, my mother beckoned

me over to the window where she was sitting and pointed outside at a captivating scene on the lawn in front of the asylum, where unearthly shadows played in the rising mist. Was this the myth of the werewolf? The moon was definitely causing a manic phase at the asylum. On closer inspection I could see that the shadows were actually foxes. Like the reports of crazed dog fights that you get during a full moon, there was hair flying around everywhere as the foxes seemed to be mauling chunks off each other. It was like nothing I had seen before, and it was entrancing to watch as the asylum grounds became covered with foxes that came out from the bushes to congregate and fight. I could also hear the sounds of dogs howling mournfully outside the asylum. It definitely was not like in the movies when the full moon appears and the havoc immediately ensues; the transformation was much more subtle than that. I turned to Mother and asked for her reassurance. 'It's begun, hasn't it, mother?'

'Yes,' she replied with a daunting look of concern on her scrunched up, nervous face. In my naivety, to put myself at ease and to ensure my safety on this potential night of the werewolf, I dashed around to each of the patients individually to ensure there were no protruding sharp finger nails or bodily hair sprouting from their bodies. As time went on the strange behaviour began, and the influence of the moon seemed to bring out the patients' wild side, triggering emotional outbursts and extreme behaviour. I was sitting in one of the wards and a dramatic tone manifested in front of my eyes as patients began to display bizarre, intermittent acts of insanity.

The psychological distress seemed to agitate the patients more than normal. It was getting very loud on the ward, and more patients than usual were gravitating towards me, so I went out into the corridor where I felt safer away from the masses behind the heavy ward door. I soon found that on that night there wasn't really a safe place in the asylum as even the corridors seemed to be alive with energy, irritability and sexual or aggressive altercations. As the tension grew, violent incidents occurred.

As I walked along the corridor I saw two patients I knew, David and Paul, who were very close friends and always seemed to roam the corridors together. I was intrigued by their unusual behaviour, arguing with each other as they stood by the window under the light of the full moon. Their loud and agitated argument seemed less rational and more impulsive; they were locked in a battle of wills over a magazine. Unusually for them, they were hurling verbal abuse at each other, and I was worried that it was going to escalate to violence. Without considering possible consequences to myself, I stepped between the two loyal friends to diffuse the situation. As I stood between them, I asked who the magazine belonged to. David, now in tears, claimed that it was his magazine – one of many which he was carrying in his carrier bag. Paul, now very aggressive and obviously angry, said that he only wanted to read the magazine.

'He has a carrier bag full of them,' Paul shouted, as he tried to get round me and grab the magazine again.

'Now, calm down,' I told him as I stretched my arms out to block his way. These were grown men and I was just a small boy, but they appeared to be slightly intimidated by my stance.

'It's mine and he can't have it,' a still tearful David insisted.

'Look you two, you are friends, best friends, you can share surely,' I said, thinking I was being the grown-up in the situation.

'No, shan't, I hate him,' David spat out.

'I hate him more,' Paul shouted like a spoilt, but very aggressive, adolescent.

'Come on you two, please, you love each other,' I reminded

them, realising that the power of the full moon was far stronger than any friendship between these two. Apparently it was also stronger than the power of the words of a small boy. As the words left my lips, suddenly from nowhere, as if some psychostimulant toxicity triggered extreme behavioural disturbance, Paul lunged past me and grabbed the carrier bag, ripping it out of a stunned David's hands. Before we could react he was strutting down the corridor ignoring my cries to return with the magazine. Right in front of my eyes there was an increase in terror and crime within the asylum; people were taking more risks and were willing to ignore the consequences.

I was left in the corridor with a very distressed David, and I tried to calm him down but my words seemed misplaced and had no calming effect on him, so I told him everything would be alright and to just wait where he was for one minute and I would be back with a solution. As quick as I could, I left David and dashed back through the heavy door into the ward. I looked everywhere but was disheartened to find there were not any replacement magazines for David. Then I had a brainwave and quickly found my mother's work bag, which she had brought to the asylum with supplies to get her through the night shift. I opened the zip and right on the top were two new, glossy magazines. They were women's magazines and far from the taste of a single white male, but when I returned to David with them, the tears stopped pouring from his eyes and his face lit up.

He hugged me tightly and then released me from his overexcited, loving grip, to then individually kiss each magazine. David's gratitude gave me an amazingly warm sensation like a volcano erupting in my stomach. It felt good that I could intervene in the mayhem caused by the full moon and the mischief that the puppetmaster was creating in the asylum, using its gravitational pull to control the liquid in our bodies, causing a tidal motion in our brains.

Eager to see everything that was going on, I walked around the asylum to see who else the moon had under its spell and controlling power. As I investigated, I noticed how the energy was bouncing off the walls of the asylum. The copied behaviour of patients would travel with such urgency around the institution, and there seemed to be a more heightened level of noise and movement than on days when the full moon did not have any control over the patients.

As I got further from the protection of Mother, I noticed that on this night many of the patients were attracted by my presence, and all who saw me wished to touch and smother me like a toddler would a teddy bear. I was used to this and it was normally manageable, but that night their need and desire for my comfort, and each other's, was overpowering. I noticed several patients in a similar position to me, being held down by other patients or overwhelmed by a larger or more aggressive individual. It was as if there was a sexual tension in the air, and although I did not understand it then, I did not feel comfortable around it.

I stopped to talk to a patient I knew well, and as we chatted I was grabbed from behind, which sent a chill through me as I knew I was in a vulnerable position, and fifty percent of my escape routes were cut off. In mid-conversation I was forced to rudely run from the clutches of the predator because I was afraid of something happening that I could not even name. The fear of the unknown threat overtook me. By the time I made it back to the door of Mother's ward, I had to stop and catch my breath. I didn't want Mother to be aware that I had been running for my life. I also had to prepare myself for the lies I would have to tell her when questioned about the missing magazines.

After I could once again breathe at a steady and regular pace, and my rosy red cheeks had returned to their natural colour, I opened the heavy ward door and returned to the safety of Mother's sanctuary. I was relieved when she didn't question me about her magazines, so she couldn't have noticed that they had been stolen from her bag, or perhaps on that night she was used to strange things happening and just put it down to the patients.

I sat on one of the chairs and watched the all-powerful beams of light from the orb hovering in the sky outside the windows. As time passed, some of the patients went to bed while others fell asleep in the chairs where they sat. I watched as the patients moved erratically in their sleep as if the puppetmaster outside in the sky was truly in control and pulling on their strings in front of my eyes. I wasn't sure whether the extra light coming through the windows was the cause of any sleep deprivation, and thus possibly making some of the patients restless. Then suddenly I was shocked out of my thoughts by Terry, who was asleep opposite me in a chair. One minute he was fast asleep, the next he implosively rose up as if straight out of a sarcophagus from death. Terry was still either in a deep sleep or the moon had taken full control of his mortal body. No sooner had he risen up and made my heart jump out of my chest, he collapsed back down in the chair and once again began a shallow snore. I locked my eyes on him in anticipation of the puppetmaster's next move, as the way this night of the full moon was panning out I didn't know what horrors to expect next.

In the background I could hear patients vomiting as if the full moon was using its gravitational force to literally pull liquids from their stomachs, just as it would control the seas and the oceans. I could predict that the staff were going to have a very busy night with the effects of the lunar cycle. I could also see staff themselves becoming stressed and moody but wasn't sure if this was because of the full moon's manipulation on them, or just the anxiety caused by the manipulation it had over the patients within the asylum. Suddenly there was an almighty crash, and as I looked in the direction of the noise I saw that a chair had fallen onto its side and had upset the table, and the pencils and crayons were now rolling in every direction to the floor. Not far behind that came another almighty thud as Patricia followed the contents of the table on to the floor. I initially thought she had taken a fall, but was soon corrected when I saw her ferociously shaking as the patients around her began to scream for help. Everyone was very distressed, but I didn't understand fully what was happening.

Mother immediately took charge and assisted Patricia, all the time trying to calm her with some reassuring words. I froze and sat there stock still so as not to interfere with the situation as it unfolded in front of me. I watched as Patricia had a seizure that lasted for what seemed like a lifetime. I watched her turn a multiple number of colours of the rainbow until finally her face and lips turned completely blue. There was also blood flowing like a waterfall from her mouth where she had bitten through her own tongue. On the outside I was as silent as a hummingbird, but on the inside I was petrified and screaming like a fire engine's siren. I didn't realise that I too was risking death by holding my breath until life returned back to Patricia's face. When I reopened the doors to my lungs there was an almighty sigh of relief as I gasped for air. I was so thankful to God, and the puppetmaster, when it was confirmed by Mother that Patricia was going to be OK and would definitely not die. To be honest, that night scared me so much that I had nightmares that I will never forget. I was left shaken up by the whole experience.

My mother must have known by the look on my face that I had heard, seen, and experienced enough of the full moon's effects on the asylum. Even though I had waited a long time and begged Mother so much to be there on this particular night, I felt a flow of relief through my body when she said the words, 'Shall I call your father to come and collect you?' I didn't want to look too eager, but I made it clear that I was happy to leave the asylum and my father should definitely collect me in the car instead of bringing the goat as it would be much quicker. Before I left the asylum, I had to check once again that Patricia's epileptic seizure had not left her suffering or even dead. I had a cheeky glance and smiled at the moon as I left the asylum; as it stared back I could feel its overpowering and magnificent smile beaming back at me.

The consequences of my visit that night left me with new concerns for my asylum friends, who faced increased perils during the full moon. From what I saw that night and the stories of other appearances of the full moon, I could completely appreciate and understand Mother's concerns – even after they had been dismissed by others as anecdotal rather than scientific. I now had a better understanding of the moon's power to manipulate the inhabitants of the asylum, and the dangers for the staff working during those unpredictable shifts. I also had a full appreciation and understanding of the importance of that moon-shaped mark that Mother religiously drew on our kitchen calendar every month – from that night on, reminding us both of the terrors and threats it truly represented at the asylum.

When I wasn't searching the asylum for werewolves and witnessing the effects of Mother Nature, my fear of the asylum corridors was also being heightened around that time by other chilling stories narrated by Mother – never witnessed by myself and barely believable, but the passion and detail in

Mother's terrifying experience would bring it all to life for me. In one such story, she was alone on the ward and all the patients were asleep. There was an eerie atmosphere that night at the asylum as there was a chill in the air that made you pull the collar of your coat up over your chin to cover your face. Mother said that fog had suddenly engulfed the grounds so much that it looked like smouldering smoke. Even the moonlight was dulled, and it struggled to shine and light up the asylum through the thickness of fog.

The fog filled the night with the colour spectrum of a dodgy, old, black and white movie. The wildlife outside the asylum was silent, as if there were a large predator on the prowl and they were all in hiding, except the owl that was high up in the oak trees shrieking a frightened warning over the dense fog. Not even the asylum was safe that night as the mist began to seep under the main doors, moving through every gap and crack in the fixing of the old and heavy doors like flour through a sieve. Mother was not sure if it was a sound in the dead of night or just a feeling that pulled her out of the ward and into one of the long corridors of the asylum. She was not even sure if she had fallen asleep and sleepwalked there, as she felt as if she had just woken up in the corridor without any knowledge of how she really got there. She scratched off some of the crumbling paint using the skin on her fingertips against the cold stone walls to ensure she was not dreaming.

There was an overwhelming chill through the air in the corridor; she felt the cold on her face, like when you stand too close to the open door of a freezer. The icy breeze drew Mother's attention to its source. As if from nowhere at the far end of the corridor, which Mother was already halfway down, covering one of the only two exits there suddenly appeared a ghostly manifestation. It was a Victorian-looking lady, wearing a long and flowing nightgown. Mother said that she could see how thin the cotton was by the transparency against the glow that she was emitting.

She was lit up like a Christmas tree, silhouetted by the cold brick. In one of the spirit's hands she held a lit and flickering candlestick in a shiny brass-looking holder, lighting her way through the asylum. My mother's eyes were drawn to the broach she was wearing on the collar of her nightgown; it shone as bright as the glare from the flickering candle she was holding. It was so grand and elegant that it could have been regal. It was difficult for Mother to pull her eyes away from the hypnotising broach, but when she did she noticed that the spirit was levitating and the long flowing nightgown was hiding where her feet should have been. Immediately, Mother froze on the spot as fresh sweat appeared on her face, and she felt an instant isolation in the claustrophobic corridor. She realised she was cut off and no one could help her.

Trembling with fear she clasped her hands over her mouth so tightly that not even the shallow sound of air would leave her mouth, in fear that the slightest noise would attract the ghost's attention. Mother told me how her stomach tightened into excruciating knots as she watched the ghost, and felt that it seemed familiar with the surrounding – as if she was regularly watching over somebody at the asylum, or possibly once lived or worked there. The ghost's face was covered entirely by long flowing hair, so Mother could not tell what it looked like until it suddenly turned its abnormally grey face to confront her. Mother could feel her heart about to leap from her chest as they were momentarily locked in a trance. The spirit then lifted her hand as if to plead with Mother, then it suddenly scrunched up its face, and my mother said it looked really concerned. Then, looking really ferocious, it floated down the corridor towards her with enormous urgency and definite intent, as if it wanted something from Mother or had a genuine warning for her.

As the terrifying figure came bounding down the corridor towards her at high speed, Mother, against her natural instinct, turned her back on the spine-chilling poltergeist and attempted to dodge the ghost's clutches with what was a rather uncoordinated escape. Leaving one of her shoes behind, she pivoted and literally threw herself down the corridor, grabbing the walls to stabilise her uncontrollably and overdramatic flight from the monster and what she feared might have ended in her death.

As she fled from the supernatural figure, her screams echoed down the corridor and around the asylum, stirring some of the patients from their sleep. Woken so suddenly, their howls and screams sounded as if they had been possessed by some demon. Mother said it sounded like they were part of some communal exorcism. She told me how the entire asylum appeared to come alive with torturous screams that were synchronised with my mother's howls. Mother told me that she only just escaped the ghost's grasp that night by making it to the front exit, which she fought to open as the door was large and extremely heavy. Finally she got it open and rushed out, slamming the door shut behind her and breathing easily again. The crisp night air made her feel safe again – well, as much as you could have in the grounds of an asylum at night.

Later, I wondered if it was a biblical moment that she had been witness to. Were our dead ancestors warning her of something even bigger on the horizon, or was it an omen of a pending disaster? Mother was left wondering whether there would be any repercussions or consequences for her running away and not taking what might have been an important warning or life-changing message from the spirits.

Mother returned to her normal life, but the experience had

altered her and left her with numerous questions – but also many answers. However, part of her was quite reluctant to go back to that corridor for fear of seeing the spirit again, but at the same time she so terribly wanted to meet her again and receive the urgent message. Mother said that she had an intense feeling afterwards that the ghost was not bad in any way, it just had a purpose that night. The way she talked about the spirit made me think she pitied or felt sorry for the soul. Mother often expressed anxiety for the good spirit who walks the corridors of the asylum, and questioned what could have happened in somebody's life to cause their spirit to be stuck in such a horrid place. I could tell by her trembling tone and her worried eyes that she was concerned that she might suffer a similar fate. She later thought that, in a way, the ghost's scariest attribute was that it made you think and question everything, even our very existence.

I found it very difficult to believe Mother's spooky story despite my youth, even though I could see what appeared to be the truth in her eyes when she told the terrifying tale. None of this prevented me from visiting the exact place where the phantom appeared whenever I could. If it was just myself and other patients wandering the corridor and nobody else was around, I would call out loud for the spirit to show itself. I would even go to the extent of closing my eyes and trying to communicate with the ghost telepathically, begging it to show itself just one more time, but it never did to either my mother or myself. Any fear that my mother felt seemed to be counteracted with the knowledge that there was life after death, but this wisdom failed to comfort my trembling anticipations when walking the corridors in the dark. With the high volume of patients' deaths happening during the night, if there ever were to be lost souls and tormented spirits I would think the asylum would be a good place for their congregation.

With all this information, danger, and excitement I was taking in and living with, I began to start noticing an aura around certain patients. I would not say they became special to me, it was just that oddities of behaviour found me drawn to them so much that I ended up being in the middle of this abnormal behaviour. I started to see clues to what I would soon uncover, the secret that would change everything for me and the country.

Chapter 3
Weapons of Mass Psychological Destruction

The environment in the asylum changed over the years and by the time I was eight, and could register what was going on, it was beginning to feel more like a prison than a place of assessment, treatment, and care for these social misfits. I could not have imagined staying there for even one night, forget a lifetime – as so many patients or those who had served in various roles there had. To put someone in an asylum today is very different from when these individuals were committed. Instead of being cared for and protected, it was quite the opposite; it was a place where abuse thrived and where human rights had been all but forgotten. The abuse was so widespread that it became the norm, and those incarcerated there had to live by different rules. I was so young, and in reality also an outsider, but even to me the care seemed alien and strange.

A mere child, but I could still see that even the most basic of needs were not met. It was definitely not a good environment for anybody elderly or with walking impairments, as the lack of staff meant that these people were neglected and what care they received was often rushed, especially when it came to mealtimes and their personal hygiene. Rather than regular visits to the toilets it seemed that staff would wait until the patient had visibly soiled or wet themselves before they were dealt with, and often not even then. I would regularly watch patients being manhandled to speed up whatever the task was. It appeared that most of the staff were as institutionalised as the patients.

The residents of the asylum would suffer these offences without complaint, and if they did get near anyone to complain it would just fall on deaf ears. Although the injustices that I would observe on so many different occasions made me angry and sad, I was forced to bite my tongue and keep quiet as I didn't think it was my place to say anything or interrupt the routine of the staff. The staff were blinded, or at least wearing tinted shades, when it came to the standards, basic human rights, and needs of these individuals. It seemed that the abuse we as a nation saw later, when other such places were exposed in the media, was just a very small percentage of what was actually happening. I was witnessing it all with my own eyes and in an institution with the audacity to have a royal name.

I would imagine the asylum as a battlefield where wars had taken place. However, instead of bomb damage, the devastation I saw was from the past and present patients' treatments and medications. Even though not always witness to it first-hand, I saw the damaging and everlasting affects it had on many individuals, and these images would stay with me forever as the images of warfare would with a soldier returning from war who had witnessed the killing first-hand, forever changed by the experience. Many of the radical treatments and medications had left the patients as mere shadows of the people they once were, or could have been, as if their souls had already left them.

You would hear threats and orders regularly, rather than affection and worship, including threats that the patient would be locked in the cages in one of the asylum's towers, or that they would be given freezing cold baths. One of the most frequent tortures would be to put patients through really nasty treatments. Small and insignificant as it seemed, the staff would not check themselves in front of me and I often heard threats such as, 'Do you want all those teeth pulling out?' This one was a favourite if a patient was playing up and self-harming by biting themselves. It seemed a strange way to care for people who are self-harming, to threaten them with more harm. I came to know 'the biters' who used their teeth as a weapon against the staff or other residents and how those teeth were then removed by force.

The staff would sometimes actually tell me how some of these things were done in the past, as if they were telling bedtime stories to a child, and so I learnt about such horrors as the mind cannot imagine outside nightmares. My imagination alone would never have taken me to the terrifying places that these stories did, places where knowledge proceeds morality and humans commit barbaric and unethical acts towards one another in the name of science. They told me how therapy was limited or non-existent, so they applied what they deemed as 'science' to the treatment of these extremely vulnerable, hidden people, who were so very easy to manipulate. Here they pushed science to its extreme limits and even far beyond by performing experiments on them to allegedly advance our knowledge.

'You should be glad you have parents,' Nurse Evil, as I had named her because she was always so stern, snarled at me when I stumbled upon her administering a beating with a sharp object to a patient's feet. 'When I first came here we had lots of little ones like you, children who had no one and were good for nothing but to offer their bodies to science. Oh, what experiments and procedures we performed on them.'

'Where were their parents?' I had asked, remembering one of the nicer, older nurses telling me about the asylum's forgotten children, individuals without a physical or mental illness.

'They just arrived. Their parents brought them to us rather than leaving them out in the cold to die,' Nurse Evil said with a huge smile on her face. 'We saved those unwanted babies, and we allowed them to be part of the future, to give their bodies so others would live healthier and better lives.'

I was too young to understand the full implications of what had been done to these children, but I knew I was very glad to have my mother in the ward just around the corner.

Over time, the catalogue of horror stories I was told only grew and any strange behaviour or incident within the asylum seemed to trigger these horrific tales. They filled my head with stories of unconsented and irreversible operations – such as lobotomies. This was done by inserting cold, metal surgical tools through drilled holes in the skull or by inserting them through the eye sockets into somebody's brain and then wiggling it until the part is severed, and that was meant to control a person's behaviour. However, I was told by many of the staff who loved to gossip that instead of helping them the experiment came at the cost of their intellect and personality. They were left to roam the asylum corridors day and night like emotionless zombies. The barbaric treatment to these individuals' brains did not stop there. They also inserted electrodes through the skull to sizzle and burn parts of the brain to prevent outbursts and the violence exhibited by the patients.

The asylum staff divulged all the incredible and extreme experiments, describing how much stress a body can go through. They explained to me how defenceless patients who were put through electric shock treatment were a perfect example of the suffering that was inflicted on many. The staff would disclose in great detail each time, often in graphic detail with physical illustrations, how these individuals were inhumanely held down on beds as a rubber contraption was put in their mouth. Then, without anaesthetic, they had electric current forced through their torso, causing uncontrollable shakes until they were knocked unconscious after their bodies had suffered many seizures. I was also told the unbelievable stories of how the medical teams induced comas using injected insulin to burn up all the sugars in their body, causing them to literally ignite from the inside out – and sometimes even causing their death. I found out that it was quite common for the patients with no relatives to be used as guinea pigs to test drugs that altered the brain's chemical balance, sedated, or just caused the patient to have more symptoms and medical problems. I would often wonder if there was any correlation between these extreme procedures, which pushed the human body to its limits, and the countless number of rooms with walls that were painted from floor to ceiling with human blood. These rooms, acting as cells, often contained a traumatised individual with fresh scars, who would be constantly on edge as if their own shadow terrorised them.

The stories of these self-harmers who inflicted the worst pain and suffering upon themselves were terrifying, but prepared me for the very worst the asylum had to offer visually. Maybe all these barbaric acts and procedures in the name of science had something to do with the number of bodies regularly found by staff in the mornings in the asylum's uninviting beds, cold to the touch like an icicle, and stiff with rigor mortis. It seemed that very often the days at the asylum would begin with the chilling discovery of a dead body, and each time I was given the shocking, but fascinating, details. Due to the sheer volume of deaths during the asylum's darkest hours, this added a little mystery and made people suggest that the Grim Reaper himself had taken up residence at the asylum, while other staff told me that perhaps the asylum had a serial killer or psychotic nurse who stalked the institution until they found their next victim.

There was always a library of the asylum's terrors with multiple genres of science fiction, horror, or suspense. There was one story that I heard over and over again from different sources – one story that scared me above all the others and was a little different.

I was told that the asylum held the country's darkest secrets, secrets that were so sinister and evil that they had to be permanently silenced. In order to bring this about, some of the asylum's patients had their throats cut to keep these secrets contained. These tortured individuals weren't left to die, but they had their voice boxes removed most barbarically, and then they were sewn up again and left voiceless and unable to communicate or divulge the jaw-dropping secrets which they held.

There was a sense of good and bad staff working within the asylum walls, and the tales of the most evil of the staff would often be used as some sort of bogeyman to frighten patients into complying with the staff. Probably the most sinister threats I would hear were those that included the threat of medication. Staff would threaten the patients with injections of medicine, shouting, 'Right, P.R.N. time.' The threats would usually be used to make the patients comply or do something they had previously refused to do, or even just to speed up their reactions. Of course, at the time I had no idea what this was, or the effects of some of the remedies forced into the veins and down the throats of patients. Whenever I had medication it always made me feel better, so I had no idea of the fog and pain that psychiatric drugs could produce.

This practice was so frequent that it did not appear very serious to me at first, but it would come to have a harsh and rapid importance to me in the not so distant future. It would go on to be something that, when I speak it out loud even now as an adult, sends shivers down my spine. These barbaric treatments of the past would echo through my soul, so I can only imagine the effects it had on the precipitant.

I would often wander the corridors playing a game in my head, imagining behind which doors were housed the secrets of the past, and the pain inflicted in the name of science or the greater good. Behind which doors were trials and experimental treatments used? In my mind I could only see pictures of Frankenstein and the kind of arrangement of scientific instruments one saw in those films. You could see the results of the use of shock treatment and other extreme barbaric procedures, as many of the patients lived in fear at the threats of future treatments.

The most obvious signs of abuse when in close contact with these patients would be that of overmedication. I am sure there must have been advances in treatments in the form of therapy and less harmful drugs, but these had not penetrated the walls of the asylum as a whole, although Mother tried her best with her patients.

For the most part, the residents still seemed to be highly dosed on medication. Much of the interaction with them was limited, not because of their mental issues but because they were so doped up. This enabled staff to control many patients at one time. It was a little frightening for my younger self, seeing patients sitting in rows rocking back and forth on chairs not designed to give much comfort, or walking around in their own worlds like zombies. The rocking seemed like built up energy that was trying to burst out of them. I would wonder if the drugs were keeping them immobile as so many of them were this way. Due to the vast number of patients compared with staff, and all the daily duties that had to be done, there did not seem much time for any quality interaction – including acts of love or comfort.

There were some amazingly talented patients in the asylum. I would sit and watch or listen to them for hours at a time. Some of their talents were like nothing I had ever seen or heard of before, except for stories made up in comics or science fiction films. I would meet many patients from different wards as they travelled freely around the asylum; some of the very able patients lived in community homes and would come into the asylum each day from the outside world.

There was one resident who had the strength of ten bears, but he was not super strong all the time – just when he got angry, like the Hulk. You knew when he was angry because his normally soft voice, hardly more than a whisper, would transform into a roar. He was a huge man, about six foot five inches tall, and of big build. It was strange for such a big person to speak with such a tiny voice nearly all of the time, but I was glad of it because we were all told that when he used his other voice we were to run, and run fast, in the opposite direction. I had already heard many stories from various sources that he could pull the large heavy fire doors from their hinges, and just the idea in my head was more than enough without having to see it.

There was another patient who to look at you would think he would be unable to do the simplest of tasks; he could not speak, feed himself, or even stand up on his own without assistance. However, I often watched as he lay on the floor just to hitch himself up, to my amazement, and spin on his fingertip whatever was within his reach. He loved to spin a metal cooking-pot lid, and I loved the whizzing noise it made as it spun. If nothing was at hand, he would remove his trainer from his foot and spin that on one of his fingers. It would amaze me how he could find the centre of balance of anything he touched. I would try to spin my shoe on my finger while touching only the bottom of the sole, but found it impossible.

The most amazing talent I came across within the asylum was the Rain-Man lady. I could give her any date in her lifetime and she would have the full schedule of what she did and world events on that day. She would start by telling me which day of the week the date fell on, then list events and answer any questions I had about that date instantly. She was a marvel to me and seemed to have almost superhuman abilities. When participating in sports at school I would think of her and the Whispering Man with super strength, and it felt like we must all be capable of such marvels. It was just a matter of opening your mind; I just had to find these abilities inside me.

I would try to run faster, jump that little bit higher, and throw further. I would wonder if this was what enabled me to go on to hold both school and district records, and become captain of various sports teams at school. Had these patients had their own positive input into my development and learning? Had they, since I was a young boy, been opening my mind to the idea that we are capable of more than that which we are taught in schools? However, the secrets within the asylum walls would be having a detrimental effect on my life soon enough.

The patients had many talents that left a positive mark on me and helped me grow into the person I am. When admitted to the asylum they were registered as idiots, their home 'the asylum for idiots'. Their mental illnesses would range from non-existent, like the forgotten children of the asylum, to the most extreme and severe. Many had epilepsy, and hepatitis was widespread. It seemed that these patients were not locked up in rooms, neglected, medicated and physically abused because of their illnesses; it was down to their behavioural attributes and actions. Many of the patients were violent towards both staff and other patients, and drug-crazed rampages were frequent due to untreated disorders or conflict. Staff dealing with these incidents and disruptive patients had their hands full, much of the abuse being done in locked rooms and cells.

These patients were treated like animals. Many doors in the asylum were locked that should not have been. I would often find myself unable to get to a certain place due to the door acting as a solid wall. Patients would be locked in rooms and kept in solitude for long periods; they would scream and self-harm while begging to be released from their temporary prison. Indifference seemed routine; staff were able to switch off as if they were machines. I was not trained in the art of switching off; instead I would absorb their pain and suffering and found the cries for help both upsetting and very alarming. They became unwanted, tortured memories that I would hold forever. I still hear the screams and sounds of patients self-harming against walls and doors, wanting freedom.

I would see them banging their feet or arms against the doors and walls, but most often it would be their heads that they smashed against the bricks, like eggs being cracked into a frying pan. They would always remain contained where they had been put whatever their complaint, which just intensified and escalated the behaviour. I was only witness to a small part of what was happening behind these walls, but the torture and torment was regular, and what I did not see I would often get to hear about.

Any care that was actually offered was often hindered by the lack of adequate staffing on the wards; each shift would appear to have its own set of rules and way of doing things, sometimes even leaving just a single member of staff caring for up to thirty patients at a time. Working independently gave staff the freedom to act and do as they wished. Many would question whether the decisions made were for the welfare of the individuals they were caring for or to make their own time within the asylum easier and less demanding.

I would later come to find out first-hand the devastation and full extent of the violence that went on in the secured units, after they were renamed 'treatment and assessment units' within the community. Giving them a new name changed nothing; the staff can still lock the same patients in rooms today – just as they did at the asylum. Even as a child, I noticed that the worst and most constant abuse was not the most obvious, but it was freely overlooked. Spending a lot of time with the patients, I saw the loneliness and neglect they were suffering daily, and this had a more detrimental effect on them than the physical abuse I would witness.

What seemed the most severe and controversial abuse, I had already witnessed, but without realising its severity or extent. The staff would regularly break official procedures and replace them with their own hushed 'asylum code'. When the realisation eventually hit me, I could barely comprehend the staff 'drugging' those they medicated. I could not get my head around the reasoning, the frequency, or the legalities of what I had been witness to.

The asylum definitely did not seem to be the sort of place in which you would hide any royal secrets. However, if they were to bury some royal skeletons then they should have made sure they were buried deeper than the royal bones a child was soon to dig up.

Chapter 4
Clues to the Dead

If I had been a little older then I may have worked it out a bit sooner than I did, but when it eventually happened it changed my life forever and set me on the path that was my fate. If you want to keep a secret, first you need to ensure everybody knows it is a secret. Over time, when the secret is old and has been whispered and told so many times, people become relaxed with it and even sloppy. I was the consequence of what happens when both these instances correlated consecutively.

Royal Earlswood used a lot of temporary staff who came from different hospitals and care homes to fill the rota when permanent staff were off sick or when wards were just short-handed. These workers were a lot more relaxed with the secrets than some of the regular asylum staff, and it would be here that the final cracks would be opened. Around eighty percent of the patients within the asylum were unable to communicate, which may seem perfect to hide a secret. However, because of the patients' mental illnesses, in some cases, the small percentage of people who were left seemed to over-communicate about a secret they didn't even know they were meant to be keeping.

Mother started going to work more and more, and so I spent even more time there and also in the beautiful asylum grounds. When I was not walking the pets, I would play in front of the main building by the royal tunnels – two sections on stone steps that arched over an opening in the ground, under which tunnels led beneath the asylum. The entrance was open, but so dark you could only see a very short distance in front of you, a few steps taking you deep underground, where the atmosphere contributed to many of my father's made-up ghost stories. I thought the name came from the tunnels being part of Royal Earlswood, but I was soon to find that this was not the case at all. These tunnels would become a significant place for me, and their mysterious history would add a level of excitement that would drive my hunger and passion.

We were not the only ones to enjoy the stunning grounds, as many of the patients seemed to find peace and tranquillity wandering through the open fields with a sense of freedom they could not find within the asylum walls. I believed that not being confined to one area, or locked away, had as positive a medicinal effect as many of the modern therapies or medications. This freedom to walk around the asylum and grounds allowed the patient to get a change of scenery and to meet up with friends and other staff on different wards. I would meet many of the patients while they were on their travels. Often they would be half naked or not suitably dressed, but this did not seem to faze them; it seemed to only affect the onlookers. If you came across them after mealtime there was a good chance they would be covered in food stains. Their ill-fitting clothes, nakedness and food-stained bodies showed that there was a clearly relaxed approach when it came to the patients' appearance within the walls, and I would later learn the full extent of this lax regime.

Within the asylum the touch of a naked woman was always preferred over the touch of a naked man. I learnt from experience that you should always fear the grip of a male at the asylum, as you never knew how powerfully and tightly they would, and could, clasp on to you. Some of the male grips felt as if their hands were adhesive, preventing any escape. The females were much weaker, and I had never felt one of their grasps that I could not escape from.

On my visits, I was often forced to play the asylum's own version of dodgeball; obviously this was an asylum so there were slight deviations to the regular rules of the game, which you would only ever witness inside the walls of an asylum. The variations began with the name; inside the asylum it was 'human dodgeball'. The next addition to the rules, and what made the challenge more dramatic and terrifying, was all to do with the balls, which you would manically retreat from to escape any contact.

This was not like the game of dodgeball that I regularly played at school and at Cub Scouts, because thankfully at school and Cub Scouts it was never required of me to dodge human testicles like it was at the asylum.

This particular incident stained my memory so much that the images still influence my life to this day. At bars I always order a vodka-Redbull, and when it arrives I slide it to the left or the right across the bar or table and call it a vodka-dodgeball under my breath. It's a minor and insignificant gesture to most, but to me it reminds me of the day I had to play asylum dodgeball like my life depended on it.

Many of the patients at the asylum frantically stripped

naked when feeling stressed and frustrated. I would feel extremely awkward and close my eyes when this happened. I am not a doctor or psychiatrist, but I could see that it was a massive release of pure distress, and usually, but not always, within an asylum a naked individual receives the attention that he or she had been so desperately seeking.

The naked adult anatomy was a horrible sight for a small child like me; it did not look normal to see all the hair in crevices. It was disgusting. I learnt quickly that certain skills were required in the asylum if you wanted to avoid any contact with a naked body, which I definitely did. I had all these skills put to the test one evening when walking along one of the corridors. Like a giant crab walking sideways into a fisherman's cage, I somehow managed to walk into a trap, which immediately closed and locked down on me with no obvious escape. Without much time to think, I became frantic. I was starting to feel claustrophobic when the trap began closing in on me even further and tightening its grip. I knew that I had to come to terms with the terrifying idea that my escape was not guaranteed this time.

There was a naked patient on either side of me and the grasp of at least one of them was inevitable and inescapable. I had regularly dodged singular naked individuals, but I was worried that having to evade two naked patients, coming from two directions, was beyond my skill set. You needed moves like a panther to escape the patients' grasp for human contact. Usually, I would fake a left, then go right. Most of the time it was easy to outsmart a naked patient with a slick move. Often my avoidance skills and abilities were not even required, as a member of staff would be there to rescue me by pulling a naked leg or arm to spin them around, allowing me to scoot past.

At times being dragged seemed like the permanent

internal method of transport for patients. Like a freight train pulling its heavy carriages, or similar to when you catch a mouse or a rat by its tail and pull and lift it and deposit it to a location outside. The staff did not have any malicious intent – usually – and sometimes the patients enjoyed it. Then there were the other times when it was too rough and was done in a nasty and unkind fashion.

On that day when I was trapped, I had one patient sprawled naked across the floor of the corridor kicking her legs and throwing her arms around, while from the other direction, a large naked male was proudly walking straight towards me. I did not have much thinking time. I may have been disillusioned, but I had seen Evil Knievel on television jumping over huge trucks on a motorbike, so jumping a naked human seemed completely plausible, if definitely more terrifying. I kept my head tilted because I did not wish to look directly at him, but I could hear the naked male's bare feet slapping on the floor as he stomped closer. My runway was closing in on me fast and the balls were headed in my direction. I was trapped in a game of human dodgeball, but with my escape route narrowing I was ready to attempt the only conceivable dodge that I could envision.

With the naked male nearly in grasping reach, I took the biggest run up that I could. I leapt into the air with faith that if I got high enough my feet would clear the horridness awaiting me on the floor – and luckily they did. As I travelled through the air I felt the naked lady's fingertips bump the bottom of my trainers, but when I landed clear of her, thankfully, both of my training shoes were still attached to my feet and I did not have to return to retrieve them. Instead, I kept running and did not look back, knowing that I was triumphant and had ultimately won the simple child's game of 'asylum dodgeball'.

Some patients took full advantage of the freedom of the

grounds as the road going through the institution was extremely quiet, the only traffic being staff cars. There were two main exits; one was where the staff houses and student nursing flats were, but the other was free of any barriers – there were no fences or gates preventing a getaway. Patients regularly escaped from the asylum, but it was often just a case of them walking until they exited the grounds. There was no perimeter fencing or gates, so patients often didn't know they were somewhere they shouldn't be. On our family days out, we often discovered them walking towards Brighton or London. It felt like Mother was never off duty.

One of the many clues that Mother knew of the royal secrets hidden within the asylum, which I would soon uncover, might have been the immeasurable number of times that we visited Buckingham Palace on our sightseeing trips to London – only a thirty-minute drive from home. Not only was our spare time manipulated by royal outings, but our home was full of royal collectables such as plates, spoons, mugs, tea towels, and even jigsaw puzzles. As a family we were all very excited by our collection of royal coins, and we would regularly order them, anticipating with excitement their arrival in the post. While other little boys were collecting football stickers, my parents had me accumulating a royal coin collection.

My parents were clearly very proud to be British, each year gathering the family together at Christmas to watch in silence as the Queen made her speech on television. Their respect for the monarchy was passed down to me and my brothers and we all looked up to the Royal family. For Mother, I thought, this was because she had actually met Queen Mary as a child. The truth was clouded in my eyes, as I always thought that the draw the Royals had for us was due to patriotism. The family was so focused on the Royals that it even influenced our entertainment choices, as we often watched films and stories of kings and queens past. Among the favourites was Robin Hood and that era, and from an early age these programmes, both subconsciously and consciously, inspired me to want to fight for good.

Before our Sunday outings we would always attend the morning service at our local church. My parents were members of the Church of England and took their religion very seriously. Some of the more able patients of the asylum would join the service, although I think they were more interested in the social aspect and being treated kindly, for a change, by the other members of our church community. The majority of the people who attended the church were friendly and did not speak down to them, as the patients were so used to. They seemed to clearly enjoy being treated with respect and the acceptance shown by these kind people. It was these patients who remained close to me as I grew to be an adult, frequently visiting us for cups of tea.

After church we would always go to the asylum for lunch. I thoroughly enjoyed meeting residents that I might not have seen during the week; it was like having one huge extended family. Even our Christmas seemed to be focused around our extended family at the asylum, sharing Christmas and making it a happy experience for the patients. Seeing them all so happy made my existence in their lives seem worthwhile. After Christmas, and for as long as was possible, these patients would carry their Christmas cards with them to show me each of them every time we met. The more able residents were clever enough to know to carry all their possessions with them at all times, to prevent the theft of items by other patients. The less able patients would often be left with no personal possessions.

I would draw pictures for the patients on request, and we

would always send postcards from our family holidays, which created a lot of excitement. On our return from our holidays those patients who had managed not to lose their postcard would greet me with their love and thanks, and they would ask me to read the cards out again and again.

I was surprised that they managed to keep hold of anything, as they did not have secure bags for their belongings. They would use whatever they could get hold of to keep their possessions safe – usually a worn or ripped plastic carrier bag given to them by a member of staff.

From a young age I noticed that the patients' lives revolved round their food and drinks. Mealtimes were very hectic and usually quite messy. Staff were often strict on the portions, and patients would queue like school children at teatimes, usually not allowed more than one cup of tea and one biscuit.

'Here is your cup of tea, Your Highness. Would you like a scone with that?' I often heard one member of staff saying sarcastically to a patient called Catherine, whom they nicknamed Tinky. She would then drink her tea in two seconds flat. I heard the same joke so many times it became the norm as I watched patients down their cups of tea as if their lives depended on it. There was always the risk that another patient would take it from them if they delayed. Patients who were able would go around tables on the lookout for any unguarded cups, which they would quickly grab and drink.

During my time at the asylum, I made many of my own observations; it became difficult not to as the goings on there were so different to my regular life. One particular day, I made the discovery that would change my life completely.

'Give us a royal curtsy or you won't be getting your dinner, Your Highness,' I once heard one of the staff tell Tinky. I never gave the jokes much thought other than to be annoyed at the staff for treating the patient so unkindly. Then, one day, I was looking at a lavish royal celebration on the television when I realised who Tinky might be, but it didn't make any sense. The only thing that did make sense was the resemblance she had to the lady on the television and the face on my pocket money.

Beneath the messy hair, dirty face and unfitting clothing I could see the royal blood in her.

Chapter 5
You've Goat to Be Kidding Me

Even as a child I felt that I had a very special relationship with fate, and I had been waiting for just such a day. It may have been all the fairy tales and mystical stories I had been read, or the films about Robin Hood and the Knights of the Round Table, but it felt inevitable to me – as if I was exactly where I was meant to be. Who would have ever believed that I was sharing my extended garden and my kingdom with actual royalty? It was both clear and heartbreaking knowing that she had been rejected and denied by her whole family for her entire life. If you were to catch her in the right light, from a distance, you could easily mistake her for Queen Elizabeth herself.

From that moment of realisation I could only ever see the royal blood in her and the family resemblance. She was one of them, but had been forgotten and left behind. Nobody in the asylum would admit anything straightaway, but I knew the answers to my questions by the smiles on their faces as my inquisitiveness flooded out.

Once I was aware of the truth, some staff became more open. With others, I would catch them out by having conversations as if I already knew the full story – their responses telling me what I needed. I did not understand how much of a huge secret she was outside those walls; within the asylum it wasn't that big a deal as everyone seemed open and relaxed on the subject, and they would even laugh and joke about it. I was made fully aware by Mother of the secrecy but not the entire scale of things. I treated all the patients as part of my extended family, but it was here that my obsession began.

After I was made aware of her story, it changed things for me. It was like being a little star-struck – as if she were a celebrity or a person of great importance. However, whether it was because she did not receive any special treatment or that I had grown up around her from the age of four, I was not as star-struck as I would have expected. However, from the moment of realisation she became very special to me.

This became an unusually stressful time for me due to my brain having been warped by all the reading material and movies focused on past kings and queens that my father had at home. Thinking of all the time I had spent with her, this Royal cousin, with my dog barking at her or my goat chasing after her, I felt that I had committed a very serious crime. I imagined that they would probably bring back old-time punishments and put me on the gallows, stringing me up by my neck for such a serious offence as attacking a member of the British Royal Family with a goat. Mother had warned me at the time that if something serious had happened with my goat we would have been eating goat curry for the rest of the month. It all made sense once I knew the truth. I realise that she was more concerned about destroying the royal murder weapon than me having yet another royal secret to carry to the grave.

It was like something out of a storybook where you get to know somebody who you later discover to be royalty. All this heightened every trip to London from then onwards – visiting royal places, buildings and monuments was never the same again. Even while I slept, she would be in my unconscious. At times I would worry myself to sleep about her safety; I would dream of her and then be with her. I had dreamt about the asylum many times, but from the day that I discovered her identity she was in all my asylum dreams. I would have a reoccurring dream that I was at a masquerade ball with the Royal Family, dancing in a grand hall under the chandeliers. On removal of the masks, the guests would reveal themselves as scary-faced monsters. I never really knew what this meant, but I began to see the Royal Family in a different light to the one I had grown up with. Our royal patient was always in my thoughts as I knew the surroundings she was in to be wrong and unfair. I was so confused by it all.

The only thing that I really understood was that she was meant to be dead and that is why it was such a big secret. A secret I should not talk about. At that young age, seeing and interacting with somebody who was meant to be dead was exciting, like something from a James Bond movie that you did not actually believe went on in real life. You could see that these secrets had been going on for decades by the way the royal member was living. To think I was now part of a secret that had come from the highest place in the country – or maybe the world. It seemed to me that even if I told of these secrets, I would not be believed. However, it opened up the door to so many questions as I grew up – questioning all the conspiracies and so-called facts throughout our history. No question was as important to me as the one that I had thrown upon my curiosity like a thunderbolt from the heavens, when I noticed what I did.

After so many years of being allowed to wonder and to learn from what I saw at the asylum, it all came crashing down around me once I knew that secret. I saw something that meant I had finally reached that limit and there was definitely no path for me to travel beyond it – well, for then anyway.

I just could not believe or get my head around what I was standing there staring at; it was like something straight out of a horror movie. It blew my mind and made me question every remaining ounce of my fragile reality, which was already holding on by a shoestring. I could not get my head around the Royal Family having this horrific and unimaginable act executed to protect their dark secrets. I tried to convince myself that all this must just be a coincidence – not knowing the pattern of coincidences I would later stumble upon. I could not erase what I had seen no matter how hard I tried to, as it was right there in front of me, as clear as day. The asylum's graphic horror stories, which I had heard from the staff time and time again, were unforgettable. There it was, on the royal cousin's throat, the scar that proved the stories I had been told – the most chilling tale of them all. Could the stories be true and it was the Royal Family who were responsible for having their own relative's voice box removed to silence her completely? Without a voice it was as if she were missing her identity, and she was left in constant danger within the asylum. It truly was unimaginable.

As soon as I questioned the barbaric act, the whole room became silent and the atmosphere altered. Suddenly, the seriousness of what I had just asked was put into perspective, sending a chill throughout my entire body. Mother told me to stop talking about it in the most furious of tones, which was very unusual for her. I had clearly found the place where Mother drew the line when it came to the secrets of the asylum. I didn't know if the gory, sinister details were too much for her, or if it was the unhealthy thoughts it left in your head about the Queen and the other members of the Royal

Family. I could see by the concern on her face that I had shocked her that day with the amount I truly knew about the horrors within the asylum.

I don't think she knew until then that I had ever even heard that horrendous story before. She just refused to answer any questions on the subject and wanted me to divulge my source. I told her that I did not remember who told me, because there was no way I was going to give up the people from whom I still had much to learn. Even though I had so much more to find out, I did feel a sense of fear. I was afraid of the repercussions for my loose tongue, but most of all I feared what might happen to Mother, what retribution she might face. The weight of being responsible for your own mother having her throat cut and her voice box removed, to then be silenced until the end of time, was almost unbearable. It was all I could think about. That day I had reached the limit with Mother, but it definitely wouldn't be the end of it. If anything it would soon be multiplied.

The Royal Earlswood Asylum was the hiding place of one of the Royals' most sensitive secrets. I had many questions and I needed to know the answers. My child's mind craved satisfaction. Many of the answers that I actually received were probably to silence me on the subject, but only encouraged my enthusiasm. After discovering her real identity and actual relationship to the Queen of England, I was no longer able to look her in the face without seeing the royal blood in her. Every time I came in contact with a bank note, whether I was at school, home, or shopping, I would be reminded of the secret I was being forced to keep. It made it harder for me not to do or say anything about this unlawful silencing of a member of our Royal Family. I might have been young, but I could understand what a huge secret I held. I knew it by the tone my parents used when they told me of the threat to

Mother's position, and as I was sworn to secrecy – forbidden to talk about the subject with any friends at school, my relatives, and even with friends at the asylum. I couldn't even tell my best friend, Daniel. We would sometimes play together after school, and even though there was ample opportunity I never talked with him about the conspiracy and the top secret life I was living. Even the lifetime bond that we made by cutting and pushing our bleeding fingers together to become blood brothers could not force me to divulge any royal secrets. It felt like being a secret agent, protecting this royal lie. The Royal cousin was never called by her actual name at the asylum; instead she was known by a name you would give to a small child or a pet.

Mother told me how the Royal cousin had been called Tinky even before Mother had gone to work at the asylum, but she was unaware why. It seemed unusual and degrading that the Queen's cousin and the Queen Mother's niece was known by a name other than her own, and without any title.

I am not sure if it was my religious upbringing or the respect my family had for the Royal Family, but I would feel very humbled in her presence, while at the same time I was conflicted by the great pity and sorrow I felt for her circumstances. Considering she was royalty I was shocked that there were no advanced security cameras or presence as there would be in place for other members of the Royal Family – especially as this royal member was at daily risk. There was nothing in place to protect her from the many incidents and regular attacks on patients going on all around her, as well as some more sinister goings on that I would soon be made aware of. The royal cousin had very limited communication with no sign or verbal language, so she was unable to speak out when she was abused or attacked. She would often make a loud noise like a shriek which would be the equivalent of 'no, stop'. She was living in the asylum with some very violent and mentally disturbed people, people with very different and more severe illnesses to her own. There were incidents of violence she would come into daily contact with, as it was impossible for her to escape the overpopulated and understaffed wards.

The royal cousin was also sharing her home with sexual predators; I would later discover these were not only other patients but also some staff. The abuse was everywhere and there was a lot of it – quite the opposite kind of place to where you would come across a member of the Royal Family. I could not comprehend why she was wearing ill-fitting, mismatched clothing just like all the other patients. You would have thought that whatever the circumstances she would have had an endless purse, giving her a few luxuries or even basics, but this was not the case. I remember questioning a member of staff over this, only to be informed that she was listed as dead so could only get clothes from patients who had died and left their belongings at the asylum.

This would excuse the rags she was dressed in, and why she never wore nice clothes or any jewellery or make-up. I think the only jewellery I ever saw her wear was either from a Christmas cracker or one of the daisy chains I would make her during the summer months. Her face and clothes were often covered with the remnants of her last meal, and her incontinence meant her clothes were often wet with urine as it seeped through the pad that would not be checked or changed frequently enough – her clothes would stay wet and unchanged for hours. Knowing this, the staff would have their own designated chairs uncontaminated by the patients. 'Don't sit there' would be a regular command to me on the wards, as I almost sat on a chair only recently occupied by a wet patient.

You would often have to dodge patients in the narrow corridors due to them being covered in human waste of some form. It would sometimes be awkward to touch or be touched by them. The way many of these patients looked, they were so obviously unkept, and it made their disabilities and illnesses seem a lot more severe than they actually were in many cases – as the future would prove. I had seen the large wardrobes where all the clothes were kept on each ward, but only realised that all the patients shared these clothes once I discovered the truth about the royal cousin. They did not even have their own sections, just one mass pile of clean clothes, from which patients were dressed at random. It seemed there was far too much work entailed in allocating each patient their own individual clothes. No wonder a lot of the garments did not fit. They were also often ripped and had missing buttons where they had been pulled off by other patients or themselves.

The standard of personal care received seemed to depend on the staff working each shift. When I was at home and the nights had grown cold and the stars came out, I would wonder who was watching over her. I only ever felt completely content when I knew Mother was with her, knowing she was safe and loved. I would always ask how she was over breakfast if I had not seen Tinky. I was conflicted because I had been brought up to both honour and respect the Royal Family, and I was now having experiences that clearly showed their lack of care or compassion for their own.

Tinky was not safe and she did not seem happy in the asylum – the life that she was born into had been stolen from her. I was only a child with a solitary voice; I was a single individual who knew the difference between right and wrong and wanted to speak out to all these adults and set my royal friend free. I wanted to whisk her away from that environment, the other patients and the staff. I wanted to take her home with me, where she would be clean and dressed appropriately. I wanted to give her back a little of the respect that she deserved and had been hijacked from her.

I was helpless, but even as a child I could feel her pain and misery, and knew the daily neglect she was suffering to be wrong. It would be a lie to say she was unable to form any bonds or have relationships because the bond she made with a child would only grow. I felt protective and somehow responsible where nobody else did. She had shown me love and affection, and would appear happy to see me and sorry to say goodbye. I was a lost child in a maze of deception and lies. I was forced to live a lie within a world that was beyond my understanding. At the same time as being taught the difference between right and wrong, I was part of a conspiracy and forced to live with this lie.

Both of my parents were in the care profession and I was brought up to care for those in need or who were less fortunate than us. I still had so many questions about how and why, and so many mixed emotions; mostly I was grateful to know her, but there was also sorrow that she had been left there. To bring a child up with this knowledge would later have its consequences.

Chapter 6
Definitely Not a Palace

To me the Royal Earlswood Asylum for Idiots seemed a strange choice of hospital for a royal to spend her life in. I can understand that maybe it was once a grand and well-decorated place, or once upon a time it was the correct decision to place her there due to her type of illness, but when I was growing up anyone looking past the beautiful grounds and stunning structure would see that it was long past its prime in terms of the routine treatment of patients and the standards of living. Growing up, the institution became so familiar to me that I became almost immune to the way of life and the code of the asylum. However, once I discovered that my friend was a member of the Royal Family, I started to become more aware of the surroundings and the standards that were suitable for a royal to be living in. I had a heightened awareness of the care that was accorded a royal legend. It became a real eye-opener for me and the start of an overpowering desire to improve and change the way this royal was living.

It was a huge shock to me that she did not get any special treatment because of who she was. She had no respect or honour shown to her, as many of the staff did not care for, let alone love, the British Royal Family. Knowing that there were hundreds of private care homes, even ones local to the asylum, even luxury ones, and knowing about all of the properties the Royal Family owned and the amount of staff employed by them, it was strange that she was in this place; it wasn't like funding would have been an issue. It seemed that the lack of contact or support by the Royal Family showed them to be ashamed to be associated with their disabled relative.

For her to have been born a royal in that environment and then to be stripped of her true heritage, for the benefit of others, appeared so unfair. It seemed unjust that the royal life and the rights she was born had been swapped for a life of abuse and fear. I found myself regularly asking 'Why?' The most brutal abuse was also the simplest: neglect. The smaller private care homes offer higher standards of living and a greater staff-to-patient ratio, meaning there is quality time to spend with the residents.

It made me so angry when Mother went to work extra shifts in one of these private care homes, to find wealthy people and even a celebrity film star's family member were being given the highest standard of care. I saw it as utter madness and it showed me the clear contrast between a noble, family-orientated celebrity with a huge heart and the cold, calculated, black hearts of a power-hungry Royal Family. I wished that celebrity had joined my cause because he more than anybody in England could have helped me to blow the bloody doors off this dirty royal secret. If I had known at that time where that celebrity would end up and what he would later become, well, let's just say I would have sent my father immediately to Ikea to buy a new round table because the tables at home were all square and wouldn't have been suitable for the gathering of honourable noblemen that I had in mind.

I could not believe that royalty could be placed in an asylum and still remain there after so many years. I could not believe she had remained in this place where it would seem her human rights had been forgotten. What I had witnessed, and was to witness in the years I spent within the asylum, would make putting royalty in such a place seem far from usual. The irony was that it was the Royal Family of the United Kingdom, the term that indicated being united, resulting from the union of kingdoms, who failed to show unity within their own family when it was most required.

As a child I seemed to become immune to the smell of the asylum, but I will always remember it. It was not that clean smell you may inhale when entering a dentist's or hospital, but the asylum had its own pungent, overpowering whiff about it. Over time, I became resistant to the visual sights I was forced to see as a child – on sight of blood I would always scream for help or run to one of the wards for assistance. There was always blood, be it because patients with epilepsy had seizures in corridors and scrapes against the walls, or the more frequent self-harmers banging heads on brickwork or biting their arms as they sat alone in corridors.

At that time in the asylum the self-harmers were not treated as they are now with helmets and other safety equipment; they were just left to their own devices. You could hear their screams as they mutilated their bodies. It was as if everybody was immune to the wailing and would ignore it. I would often have to dodge patients due to them having blood on them, and often they were even covered in faeces or urine. It was usually the same patients who would be in this state, and I had to learn very quickly which ones they were. Usually their hands, which would reach out for my affection, would be in the same dirty state, so I was forced to learn fast how to avoid them. I would often be warned of hepatitis and other such diseases I could catch, so I was very aware of the importance of washing my hands and keeping myself clean of the asylum's contaminations.

One evening at the asylum, as my whistling echoed against the walls of the corridor, I was suddenly interrupted by several patients who I discovered to have blood splattered across their clothes. There was no way of knowing who or where the blood had come from, and their impatience, which would not allow them to stand still for long, made it near impossible to inspect them for any fresh cuts and wounds.

My eyes were drawn to the floor, and as I looked down I discovered traces of blood, which I followed. I began to feel that the pressure was on, while also concerned about what and who I might find. The blood trail eventually led me to a patient who was entirely oblivious and unconcerned that she was covered from head to toe in blood. The amount of blood made it look like her body had been thrown into a food blender. She looked as if she had just barely survived a massacre. She refused to stop touching the wound on her head, which meant she was continuously covering her hands and clothes in more and more blood. It was like she possessed the Midas touch, but rather than everything turning to gold, everything she touched turned bright red with blood.

The blood mixed with urine was scattering like a red firework that had exploded across the floor. A crowd of patients were gathering, trampling in the blood and spreading it even more.

'Help, help, she's dying,' I yelled until somebody came running to the rescue. It was one of the male nurses and he looked really concerned as he saw the river of red. He instantly inspected the patient for cuts and wounds that could account for the massive amount of blood. She moaned aloud as he briefly lifted her top up and then checked her legs. 'I think she has a gash in her head,' I said, thinking it was quite obvious where the blood was coming from. He frowned at me and then started combing through her hair with his fingers.

'There is a tiny cut,' he agreed. 'How did this happen?' he asked the woman, which was odd as even I knew she was non-verbal. 'They can't keep out of trouble for a second,' he moaned as he pulled the woman up by her arm and dragged her down the corridor. I never saw her again, and the matter of the blood in the corridor was to remain forever one of the asylum's many mysteries.

I wasn't too worried for the woman, as serious injuries were usually dealt with immediately; it was human rights where the asylum was lacking. The way the staff seemed to treat these individuals as they pleased illustrated to me how this royal figure in my life had her human rights stripped from her with her incarceration. Prisoners in the criminal justice system had more rights and privileges than the royal prisoner of the asylum. I would often wonder why she had been put in a place like this. It was hard for me to understand what the reasoning could be for that privileged life to be taken from her. Things could have been so different and the complete opposite to where she was. I could not see how the Royal Family could not have swapped some of their drivers, cleaners, chefs, dog walkers, personal assistants or butlers for a team of carers and enabled the royal cousin to live the life she was born into.

I can say without any doubt in my mind that the royal cousin was not placed in the asylum and declared dead for her benefit or safety, as she lived a life of daily risk, abuse and neglect. It seemed to me that the placement at Royal Earlswood by the Royal Family was for their own benefit. I could not find a single reason for the monarchy to lie and say one of their members had died, which was the case with Tinky, given the possible ramifications. Should she have even been allowed to be put in a state-funded asylum when she was from such a high-income home? It must be one of the very rare times in which royalty would use such state services. I guess it did not worry them much because as far as they were concerned she was dead.

It would seem to me that the love for power had overcome the power of love. I do not believe that the Royal Family did their best, or even tried at all to help her, as from what I saw they just lied and did nothing but continue to deny her existence. It was my experience that you don't know what people with difficulties are capable of until you give them a chance, and we should all get as much opportunity as is possible. People who have no legs climb mountains; people with no arms swim and drive cars. We are all capable of much more with the help and support of our loved ones. Suffering from an illness alone is difficult and unmotivating.

After the discovery of my royal friend, I began to realise the full extent of how impossible it was to live in the asylum. I would often get lost within the tall, plain, cold, stone walls. Where there was a rare window, you would often find it decorated with a curled-up patient on the windowsill, like a cat sitting by the window wanting to go out.

After watching Superman on the television at home, it was my and every other child's dream to have superpowers similar to those of the caped crusader. Having hot lasers shoot from my eyes, amazing strength and speed, or to have X-ray vision would have been very useful traits in the asylum.

It would have also been useful to shield myself and the devastating information that I held, now that I had been recruited for the dangerous mission of guarding and protecting the nation's darkest royal secrets.

However, one day I discovered that I had my own superpower to match the amazing abilities and mesmerising superpowers of many of the astonishing residents of the asylum. It hit me suddenly like a bolt of lightning; it was completely unpredicted and my new abilities felt overpowering. I never expected to be blessed with such breathtaking powers. It was both shocking and exciting, like finally discovering the *Titanic* at the bottom of the ocean. Once I had the superpower, it remained with me. It was forever on my mind and I could not help myself overthinking all the possibilities. I became more and more aware of my amazing capabilities, but at the same time I was humbled by the asylum itself.

I was grateful; it was the asylum that had empowered me with these superpowers and the subsequent satisfaction of being a real-life hero. Like many of the superheroes, I had to keep my powers a secret. Superheroes are often misjudged, leaving a hero looking like a villain. It was literally a punishable offence to use my superpower, so I had to keep my identity a secret, being covert and very careful to never be caught. That is the reason this superhero did not wear a cape. Sometimes possessing a superpower is not all that it is cracked up to be. As much as it was a blessing, I eventually found that it could be a painful and distressing hindrance to hold such powers.

One evening I walked down the corridor unannounced, straight into an apocalyptic battle. Brian, who was known to be a wild patient who lacked decorum, was groaning loudly with blood dripping down his head and onto his face. He was clearly distressed. My presence momentarily paused the devastating violence, which had levels of aggression like I had never seen before, but after just a split second of tranquillity the fight continued. I placed my hand over my face to cover my eyes and peered through the gaps between my fingers; I could barely watch the barbaric attack. The uncontrollable temper could have led to anything, and the sheer level of aggression and violence made me believe that somebody was going to end up dead.

Kicks and punches were being thrown repeatedly. I could see wounds opening up and erupting in bright-red fountains of blood, splattering across the walls and floor of the asylum. Suddenly, Brian opened his mouth wide to reveal his unkept teeth, then he launched himself forward to take a very different approach to the volatile attack by showing a multitude of devastating fighting skills and techniques.

I watched as he attempted an unusual and unpredictable approach by biting at his opposition in the wildest of manners. It was as if I were ringside watching a Mike Tyson boxing match. Now gripped tightly by Brian's teeth, the two opponents were locked in a violent cage fight that neither could escape. As this was happening within the asylum, one could say it was a 'cage within another cage' fight.

Brian's defenceless victim was a hard and heavy fire door – one of the heaviest in the asylum. The mighty door was acting as a barricade, trapping and preventing him from getting to where he wished to be – out in the grounds. Brian was snarling through his gritted teeth and biting at the door handle without any consideration for his own dental care or hygiene. Eventually, after the pounding did not have the desired effect, Brian surrendered the handle of the door and began repeatedly whacking his head on the main body of his wooden entrapment, like a woodpecker chipping away at the bark of a tree.

At times I wasn't sure whether he was trying to break through the door or just ease his own tension through self-harm and severe pain. Suddenly Brian stopped the attack, as if reason had returned, and stared at me straight in the eyes; then without words Brian begged me to release him from his imprisonment and his captive state. Brian's lack of vocabulary was not because he was obeying and upholding the first rule of fight club; instead his voice had been taken at birth due to a disturbance of the brain. I just wanted to stop the distress and all of the unnecessary bloodshed. I had a very tough decision to make, and I stood there torn by the choice. Having these immense powers came with immense responsibilities. I turned around to look behind me and saw that nobody was around. It was a safe environment for me to openly exert my superpower and be the hero. This was the perfect opportunity for me to erase his distress and pain by using my secret 'healing' abilities, and the instant relief was exactly what was required; luckily for Brian, that was my superpower.

By covertly opening the doors I became the secret hero of the asylum. This power I often employed after the discovery of a patient who had been abandoned at a doorway in an intense state of distress, and after checking that nobody was around. I would regularly open the internal doors of the asylum for those who were forbidden from entering certain areas – erasing their pain and distress in an instant. It was such a simple task but brought immense joy and relieved the patients of some of the pain and torture that the asylum offered them each day.

That day I held the power to offer Brian instant relief from the obvious distress and pain that he was causing himself, but at the same time the door he wished to travel through was one of the extremely heavy external doors and passing its threshold may have led him to even more danger. I could not stand there when he was bleeding, hurt and in so much distress, but at the same time I could not open the external door and possibly lead him to a worse fate. I had to turn my back on Brian and walk away, desperately trying to drown out the sound of his head pounding on the solid door and his cries of distress. That day I learnt the immense responsibility and exactly how tough it was to be a hero. After spending time in an asylum I realised that we all possess superpowers and have the ability to be a hero, but every day we choose not to use them and remain ignorant to the happiness and amazing possibilities that simple acts create.

There was no sign of any previous heroes trying to stand up for Tinky at the asylum because the royal cousin's ward, where she would be found when not strolling the corridors or in the day centre, was very cold with next to no soft furnishings, no ornaments or framed pictures – as these would be taken or destroyed by the patients. None of the chairs matched and the furnishings looked like they had been picked up at a garage sale. The television was always switched on but was housed behind a protective plastic screen built into the cabinet. The plastic shield always seemed to have something splashed or smeared on it; there were patients who would, as if by habit, smear their food or their body fluids while passing by.

You would often hear a scream of 'stop' from a member of staff if a patient was caught in the act, but the behaviour would soon be repeated. Her sleeping area was even more depressing than the main living area. All the beds were lined up in the room, giving her no personal space; no personal items of any value were to be seen, as these would only be lost in the day. Instead of sleeping in a private bedroom, she was forced to share a room with other patients she did not get on with. I would sit on her bed with her and I can only imagine how uncomfortable she was when she slept. The metal beds, with their thick plastic mattresses, hospital sheets and pillows, were uncomfortable to sit on for even a short time.

It would bring tears to my eyes to see the grand and lavish rooms the royals frequented on television, knowing that selling just one of their paintings or vases could change the Royal cousin's life. I was not looking for her to be put up in Buckingham Palace, just to be removed from the hell that she was living in. The only things that were pretty or nice in her life were the views outside the windows, but I was not sure if that was a luxury or even more torture. I would lie awake at night and appreciate my own surroundings at home, at the same time being sad for the royal who lay in a cold asylum.

It was interesting to see how the other patients interacted with her, having no idea of her status. She would often be pushed around by others due to her slowness and lack of mobility. There were a handful of patients who were aware of the identity of the royal resident and would talk about her at great length, but it was just repeated information and not an understanding of her importance or secrecy. There was one lady, Anna, who was in a wheelchair, who would at times show genuine emotion over the treatment of the royal patient. They had spent their lives together in the asylum, and Anna would explain what went on in great detail; she also had an amazing memory so no details were forgotten. The patients' behaviour towards the Royal cousin could be excused by their illnesses or the conditions that they were being kept in, but I began to notice the staff would treat her in a way that was humiliating, abusive and embarrassing – and shameful to be witness to.

Every day I wondered if someone would come and take Tinky from the life that she had not chosen. With more support her life would have had meaning, I am sure of that. In the asylum it was just a matter of control; they didn't have the staff to watch or entertain her needs. I would often watch her just sitting staring at nothing in particular, and wonder how she perceived the world she lived in. What was she thinking?

I guessed that the fact that she did not have family photos or pictures was due to the need for secrecy, but I could not understand her lack of possessions and any luxuries. Beneath her grime I could see her royal blood, but dressed as a pauper with no personal belongings, one could start to question her true identity. I could only describe it as like finding Tarzan in the jungle. When you think of royalty you imagine a figure with fine clothing and jewellery, but instead she was in rags with nothing of any significance to show. She loved to be visually stimulated and the lack of environmental stimulants was clearly detrimental to her.

I can remember the unimaginative food she would have each week. I know that her condition would mean that she would be lost when it came to choosing the right cutlery to use at a royal dinner table, but to have a wider choice of meals would have been a real luxury compared with the minimal choice she had over the decades. I would watch as the meal trollies came round to each ward. Large trays of covered food would arrive and you could see the excitement on the patients' faces. The Royal cousin would eat at the dinner table, unlike others who ate where they were sat. Others gathered around the meal table, and at times it would become quite a battle.

The Royal cousin would nearly always have her food tasted by others before she ate any. This would not be to test for poison, as was the custom of old when royalty had official food tasters – it was just due to other patients grabbing at it in desperation. It was an unusual, if not impossible, sight in the outside world to see a royal begging for food and cups of tea, and regularly eating scraps from the floor, but it was very normal behaviour within the asylum. The more I thought about the lavish lifestyles other royals were having, with excessive funds, property and staff, I became even more aware of the unfairness of it all. She was born into this life with all the power in the world and it felt so wrong to witness her live the lifestyle she did in this secret kingdom. It seemed to me that I was caring and doing more for my goats than the support she was receiving from her family or anyone outside the asylum walls. I could not imagine having all the means in the world and yet not helping a member of my family who needed it, especially when the Royal cousin's illness was not of her making but a matter of genetics. I sometimes wondered if that was what the royals wanted to hide, their genetic secret.

To be honest it should not have been a how, why or who question to remove the Royal cousin from this life of daily abuse – it was beyond that. It should have just been done immediately for the safety of a member of the British Royal Family. Perhaps she should never have been put in that position in the first place. She had nothing royal in her life; she had nothing of any real meaning. I could not comprehend how her existence could be denied and rejected by her family like this. To watch this royal figure being forced to live this difficult and empty life in this 'school of hard knocks', learning by her own mistakes and not given the appropriate support, was beginning to make a real impression on me. It would change my life.

I began to see her differently to the other patients; she was royalty to me, and I felt it to be my duty and honour to protect her. She was not only a part of our English history as all Royals are; she was a human being with an awareness of her surroundings. She should have been seen as an equal and have an equal role, according to her ability, within the Royal Family and our society, without being registered as dead and hidden in an asylum. Happiness is supposed to be the highest good, and to gauge how happy a person is we look at their whole life, not just moments within it. I wanted to do more for her than just those moments of happiness that we shared. However, as I came to realise, within the asylum it came second to survival. She did not ask for all that I did for her, or comprehend all that

I could do, but we still shared some desires and rights – the desire for food and water when we wanted it, shelter and companionship, freedom of movement, and the avoidance of pain. These basic desires were not being met to any kind of standard you would expect for royalty, or any other human being. I was going to have to make some changes around here.

Chapter 7
In Training

I was obsessed with the welfare and happiness of my royal friend. Though I could not talk about her or discuss my own unhappiness or excitement, the need to was intense, as Mother did not like me to talk about the dark, secret part of her life. This just ignited and encouraged the inquisitive side of me. I wanted answers to this mystery, this injustice. I had greater expectations of our Royal Family, the working members of which seemed to do so much work for charity and raised so much money for good causes. I expected somebody to come for her. I thought that one day she would just be gone as secretly as was her existence. I would imagine it being done by helicopter or that a fleet of vehicles with their windows blacked would arrive in the dead of the night. However, time went past, and my excitement grew whenever there was a royal birth or wedding, thinking this would be the occasion they would relent and embrace their cousin – but nobody ever came.

For no apparent reason, she appeared to have become the target of abuse, and I constantly wondered why, if she had to be institutionalised, she was not sent to one of the good private homes close to us rather than being left in this abusive environment. The way she was dressed and the state of her personal hygiene was inexcusable and baffling to me.

I had nobody to answer all the questions I had. I could not grasp the ignorance shown by such a noble family. I wanted something to change for the better in her life, and I was determined to be the one to make it happen.

From the moment I learnt this secret, my family holidays and even days out were full of guilt, thinking then overthinking how the royal would enjoy being outside the asylum – but, of course, with the appropriate care. I felt guilty for the life I was having and the life she had been deprived of.

Then there came a point when I was no longer able to keep my concerns to myself – a mistake that I would later live to regret. I questioned the staff about the Royal cousin's next of kin, and asked who the royal in charge of her care was. I was told that there was a London-based solicitors' firm to which any correspondence was sent. There was never any direct contact with the Royal Family. This only added more mystery to the already unbelievable.

Not being able to talk with anybody about my feelings and emotions, and now being part of the conspiracy, began to wear on me, so I started to write down my worries and concerns. I must have practiced over a hundred times before I wrote the letter for real. I think it may have been the constant visual stimulant of the bright-red postbox at the end of our drive; it seemed to be calling to me each day like a beacon. Knowing Mother would be furious, I wrote in secret. I wrote about my sadness and concerns for a member of the Royal Family.

Writing a letter to the Queen may have been stupid and may have had some serious consequences, but at the time I didn't give it a thought, nor would I have cared if I had. I was determined to help my friend, so I wrote an unsigned letter addressed to the Queen at Buckingham Palace. I wrote about her cousin's clothing and the poverty she was living in. I also informed the Queen about the abuse. I only put half of what I witnessed because I feared retribution on Mother for being responsible for letting the secret out. I can remember the fear and anticipation when finally posting it. I was so scared that Mother would find out but something in me gave me the strength to continue on my mission.

I was expecting my response to come in the form of a change in the care that she received, but nothing changed and the abuse continued. It felt like I was the only one who cared enough to want change. I may as well have written a letter, placed it in a bottle and thrown it into the sea. I never thought that this innocent letter could really cause any serious damage or consider whose hands it could end up in.

Living so close to the asylum made it easy for me to get to my new, self-appointed post. I would ride my blue BMX bicycle around the grounds as well as the main and outer buildings, checking security. I found it so strange that there was no security in place for their royal resident. She had no bodyguards, security dogs, and absolutely nothing had been put in place to ensure her safety. Even at night there was only one single member of staff watching over her and a ward full of other patients. It concerned me that anybody had access to her as there were no gates or even security cameras. I often saw people I did not know and I would follow them, spying from afar, ensuring that they were not going to where she was. When there was nobody to spy on or follow, I would do my security checks of all the outer buildings, but little did I know that the real dangers she needed guarding from were within the asylum walls.

There were many different buildings within the grounds, but none of them scared me as much as the mortuary. Mother would tell me stories of deaths, which seemed to be very frequent at the asylum – possibly due to the age of the patients. The mortuary was a different colour from the other buildings and you could feel what seemed like an aura of death around it. The further into the grounds I would go, the higher the anxiety and fear, especially at night. I would complete my rounds by visiting the units holding the violent and dangerous patients, which were furthest from the main building. I would often stop to watch the patients through the wired pen they were kept in, and listen to their screams, but kept a good distance because in my head I had this fear of being eaten alive by them.

One night as I reached these buildings the moon suddenly disappeared behind a cloud and it was pitch black. Stopping still, my legs shaking too much to ride my bike, I felt a presence nearby. As I tried to listen to see if I could hear it approaching me, suddenly there were blood-curdling screams coming from one of the buildings. I knew that the worst was about to happen to me, and so I tried to jump on my bike but I was so scared I just crashed to the ground, my bike trapped between my legs.

That's when I felt the hand and I knew I was about to die.

'Don't,' I screamed, hardly recognising the terrified voice that came out of me. 'I am your friend, don't kill me, I pleaded. 'I come here every night to protect her.'

Knowing how little some of the patients within the asylum understood, I held out no hope for this king or queen of mental disease.

'Don't ye worry lad,' came the voice as a set of hands dragged me to my feet. 'I'll no hurt ye, it's protecting them that brings me here every night.'

I was not one hundred percent sure, but I was alive and in

possession of all my limbs, so I shouted 'thank you' to the dark figure and ran, dragging my bike beside me.

It had been one of Mother's rare nights off, and next morning over breakfast I casually asked her, 'Mum, how many guards are there in the asylum grounds at night? Lots round the units holding the violent and dangerous patients, I bet.'

'I wish we had the money for that.' Mum laughed. 'No, at night the grounds take care of themselves. Just as I was to ask another question, the telephone started to ring and Mum answered. She was mostly silent, just saying 'I see' a couple of times.

When she put down the phone, she looked at me in a strangely suspicious way. 'Did something happen last night?' she asked me. 'Did you see anything from your window?'

Little did she know, but I just denied everything and quizzed her about my question concerning the guards. I just pretended I had been wondering about escapes for some time.

'I am so sorry you feel so frightened, my darling, and I want you to know that in this house you will always be safe. The fact is, one of the most dangerous of our patients somehow got out last night, and no one can find him.'

'How dangerous, Mum?' I asked.

'Don't you worry, they will catch him soon. He used to be a nurse here, but the pressure of working in those units sent him over the edge and he has been a patient for thirty years.'

'Why is he dangerous?' I asked again.

'Oh, you will be safe, darling. Big Matt only attacks patients who try to hurt other patients, ones that can't defend themselves. I've wanted them to move him to the normal wards for years, but when they try he gets very angry, so he has been left with the most violent and dangerous people,' Mum explained.

It was at that moment that I realised I had met a kindred

spirit, another defender of the vulnerable at the asylum. Big Matt was never found, but I could often feel his presence late at night on my rounds.

It was nice to be near the staff social club, which was also within the grounds, as I felt safe being where somebody could hear my screams if I was attacked or grabbed. All the night staff would meet at the social club before their shifts and have a drink and a chat. It meant nothing to me at the time, but now looking back, having alcohol was not the best way to start a night shift, especially when you were caring for royalty.

I remember the staff would sit together, many of them drinking pints of Guinness and laughing. I would have judo classes in the evenings at the club then have time to spend with the royal cousin until after the evening medication had been given out, when my mum would have a break and take me home.

I had never in my life seen a dead body before, so one evening following a judo session, I had a petrifying awakening. After my session I left the judo club and with a happy skip in my steps I ambled slowly through the grounds, taking in the pleasant atmosphere. My face was glowing as I anticipated seeing Mother and telling her and the patients about all the judo moves I had been taught.

'Wiiiiyyyaaaaaa,' I screamed as I jumped in the air and burst through the door of the ward, landing on my feet with my hands held up in an attacking posture in a karate stance. Mother heard me and immediately yelled out 'stop right there', refusing to allow me to attempt any of my new judo moves on any of the patients, even though they were all eager to learn. You could see the disappointment all over their faces when I was forced to coach them without any physical contact. I was still in full white costume from my judo lesson. They acted as if it were like nothing they had seen before, even though most weeks I appeared on the ward in the same outfit. One patient asked if I was wearing my pyjamas, so I had to quickly silence the laughter by showing off a few of my fighting techniques. I threw several punches and launched myself through the air with some flying kicks that were not even taught during my judo lesson, but the patients did not care.

Whooshing behind me was my colourful judo belt, flapping behind my body as if the Red Arrows had just attempted a flyby leaving a brightly coloured smoke trail. I lunged forwards and backwards in both attack and defensive positions, like they did in the movies. To make it even more authentic I shrieked in what I felt sounded like the oriental fighting noises that I had seen in the movies.

I had learnt many of the moves from kung fu films on the television, but I would tell the patients that I was a kung fu master who had learnt his skills from a Chinese monk in some remote mountains. My biggest downfall, and what I would quickly learn to regret, was when I told them that I was there to teach them how to fight off any personal threats and all of the other dangers that the asylum had to offer. It was never my intention, but in hindsight maybe I placed patients at risk and I was slightly to blame for some of the violence within the asylum, after coaching my chosen few in the art of judo and kung fu.

The ward quickly filled up with laughter and groans of joy, but I noticed that one patient was ignoring my performance and showing no interest in learning the new martial art techniques. As I moved towards her I could see that she looked awfully pale and her body was flopped to one side over the arm of the chair.

I watched as fluid seeped out of her mouth and travelled down the side of her face, while vomit – or the remainder of her dinner – was dripping down the front of her clothes. Her deep blue eyes were wide open and staring straight back at me, making the whole experience even more terrifying. I clapped my hands loudly several times in front of her face but got no reaction from her lifeless body. I had heard that people implode internally when they die, and that was just what it smelt like when I went closer to her. The pungent smell forced me to hold my nose; it was obvious that the unmistakable smell of urine and death was in the air. It took a moment to take everything in and register what had happened. I got nearer and looked for any movement to show she was breathing, but I saw nothing.

There remained hope in my heart that she was just sleeping, but when I lifted her heavy arm and released it, it became a dead weight and dropped like a ton of lead. I probably should have checked closer for a pulse, but I was far too petrified to touch a lifeless body again now that I was convinced. Instead I screamed and continued to scream, immediately silencing the whole ward of frantic patients. I went into a state of shock; I felt light-headed, like I could drop to the floor at any moment. I did not wish to make a scene, but it was impossible not to when you are staring at a dead body with its eyes fixed and wide open, staring straight back at you like she had died in a state of shock.

Mother had briefly left to get something from another ward, so even though I cried out for help, she could not hear through the enormous fire doors separating the ward from the corridor. I took off like a racehorse being released from the starter gate at the Grand National. 'Help, help,' I yelled while running to get as far away from the ward as I could. To my surprise, I found myself at the door to the ward where Mother had gone, and as I looked up I saw two extremely concerned individuals looking shocked and very worried.

Next to my confused Mother was Geoff, a member of staff

who, once I had told him frantically what I had found, instantly took off running down the corridor towards Mother's ward. Mother and I chased after him but could barely keep up. As we approached the lifeless body I shouted, 'Was she murdered?' I saw that Geoff was also having trouble finding any signs of life. It looked like she had been beaten over the head and left for dead. I just prayed that I was not to blame and it was not the devastating result of one of the patients imitating one of my flying kicks or other kung fu moves on her.

Mother demanded that I leave the possible murder scene immediately. I slowly stepped backwards away from the crime scene, but as I did I saw Geoff check for a pulse, and then it happened. Life seemed to leave our bodies momentarily – me, Mum and Geoff – as we all jumped out of our skins as the lifeless body exhaled an almighty gasp of air.

'Call off the coroner, it's just the effects of her medication,' Geoff said, with a look of utter relief across his face. After our living-dead patient came back to life I was a little embarrassed to say the least, but it was an easy mistake for a child to make. This happened again and again, but after witnessing the powerful and overpowering use of these antipsychotic drugs at the asylum, instead of worrying I learnt to recognise the look of a drug-induced semi-conscious patient. Some would say this was just a rehearsal, as this was not going to be the last individual at the asylum whom I would be bringing back from the dead.

As the unofficial Royal Guard in training, my other self-appointed duty was to spoil the Royal cousin as often as I could, not just with sweets and treats but also affection. I discovered that at times the best way to her heart was through food. In a place where comfort and luxury had been forgotten, she would always be happy and show gratitude for the simplest of pleasures, small inexpensive gifts and treats –

especially for things I would take for granted, such as comfort, acceptance and amusement. It was extremely difficult to sneak in chocolate for her as the mess she made would always give my secret mission away.

When Mother was at home, I would get her to bake cakes and biscuits for me to take to the asylum and share out. My birthdays and Christmases were especially good times for having ample treats with which I could spoil my royal friend.

She was clearly out of place and far from the environment that was her birthright. We would have our own royal tea parties with cake, cucumber sandwiches and as much tea as she could drink. These were often disrupted by grabbing, uninvited guests, who the Royal cousin would love to shoo off – she did not always like to share. She was very British and loved her tea. I often took my dinners onto the ward and shared them with her. She ate the fries and bit into the burger – was this the first member of the Royal Family to eat a McDonald's?

I would even entertain her by taking in my guitar and recorder to stimulate her, play music and dance with her – which she loved – but it was affection and human touch that she desired more than anything else. I would comfort her and give her cuddles and she would often not want to let go. It was horrible when it was time to say goodbye, worrying that without me there was no one to look out for her. I really wanted to take her home with me so that she would be safe and protected. I wanted to make her look and feel comfortable, even if it was for just a short time. The figure in front of me who resembled royalty, and had their blood flowing through her veins, seemed just a small portion of what she could be.

I begged Mother to let me spend my pocket money on buying her some clothes; this did not take too much persuasion as I think Mother felt the same way. We would go to charity shops and if there was anything suitable and not too expensive, I would purchase it for the Royal cousin. It would make me so happy to see her wearing the clothes; she would look amazing for a change and her face would light up. I also bought her a few little gifts when Mother allowed it. This would make me appreciate what I had, and I was grateful for the family and friends I possessed in my simple life.

All she wanted was some peace and to be free from irritation or violent attacks. The more time I spent with her, the more I began to realise the extent of how cut off she was from her family. I felt like I was her only true and loyal friend. I seemed to be the only companion she had who was not paid to be there. It felt like the more you put in, the more you got back in return, and we were able to have a meaningful friendship. I was more like family to her than her real Royal Family had ever been. The love was reciprocated; she loved our interaction and thrived on treats and affection. My free time was spent with her and I became infatuated with both her and the lie. I began to track her and watch her routine the best I could. I even had a notebook in which I kept notes about her movements. I started to see patterns and notice things that others thought I did not see or hear. The worst abuse was happening regularly, right in front of me, and I did not even understand or comprehend what it was yet. I was too young to realise it, and my youth blinded me to what was happening within the walls of the asylum.

Chapter 8
Just Routine

Spending time at the asylum was becoming a real eye-opener. I never knew what to expect. I was mixing with members of a community who were always truthful; it was as if they had lost the need to lie. None of the patients hid who they truly were; it didn't matter if they were a sexual deviant, a pervert, a flasher, a sexual exhibitionist, paedophilic, or a thief – they were all openly flawed individuals. I became used to hearing bad language, seeing naked men and women, angry and aggressive patients, and the sight of blood, urine and faeces was becoming less of a shock. I guess part of me was becoming as institutionalised as the staff. As I began to take more interest in my royal friend, I saw more of the pattern of abuse and neglect that went untreated and was even accepted.

The patients would be woken up abruptly each morning, sometimes when it was still dark. There would be so much to do on the ward each morning, with a whole ward of patients to get up, help to the toilet and shower, then dress before their breakfast turned up on the trollies. It was very loud and frantic in the mornings due to the lack of staff and the workload. You could hear the moans and screams of tired elderly people being shaken out of beds, or being impatiently herded like cattle from bed straight to bathrooms.

In the evening the medications came around to the ward at about nine o'clock. I would sit on the ward as the medication was organised by the qualified nurse, and it would be given to patients and the forms completed. I would also watch as they left the 2 a.m. medication at the same time so that they did not have to make a return visit.

The patients did seem to be treated as animals at times, not equals. I thought that they were treated in the same way as we would hustle our goats into their shed at night when we would shut them in and away from the foxes.

This treatment was not for the patients' safety, it was because of time restraints. The patients were often manhandled, depending on who was working the shift, as some staff were more hands-on than others. I did not yet realise then, as I do now, the full extent of this physical abuse. As a child I would watch the Royal cousin and other patients being shouted at and manhandled. At the time, I even accepted that these people had to be treated and spoken to in this way, thinking it was the only method to control them. I did wonder why it seemed only to be a small portion of the staff that used these very physical tactics, but at the time accepted it when it went on so openly. I did not realise the full extent of the physical abuse in the asylum, as it was profuse and became a habit for many of the staff. The closed off environment allowed staff to become relaxed in their behaviours. There were some caring staff, but they seemed outnumbered by the abusers, so patients were regularly treated like prisoners or animals.

One day, at dinner time, I was sitting on the ward like the Invisible Man, watching the world go by, and the Royal cousin's meal looked untouched. The shift leader, Rachael, came over to the dinner table and began to clean and clear away the dirty plates, including the Royal cousin's untouched meal. As Rachael lifted the Royal cousin's plate to throw away her uneaten food, Lorraine, another staff member, protested and said that the Royal cousin would eat her meal with a little bit of coaxing.

'She had her chance. If she decides not to eat, that is not my problem, Rachael said. 'No food, no dessert, Your Majesty,' she sneered.

'I said leave it,' Lorraine, who had been dealing with another patient, shouted as she pulled the full plate out of her colleague's hands.

With the Royal cousin's dinner plate now tightly gripped in her hand, Lorraine continued, 'Don't you have a heart? All she needs is a bit of patience, some help and a boat load of empathy,' Lorraine said, her voice shaking, as it took guts to confront Rachael, a highly ranked member of the asylum's secret society.

'Why should she get special treatment? She is driving me nuts, with her airs and her fuss over everything,' Rachael justified to Lorraine, before turning her anger on the Royal cousin. 'You are not special here, there are no silver spoons and I am not your lady-in-waiting. I am sick of cleaning up after you. Eat what everyone else eats or go hungry.'

Watching this confrontation, I realised that this secret was not as much of a secret as I thought; Rachael was in on the conspiracy and I guess so was Lorraine.

Watching this verbal battle, it came to me that even the staff who began with good intentions grew to dislike the patients they were taking care of, even growing a resistance to their care needs. I continued to listen as the volume of Lorraine's voice rose, and with a tone of authority she explained how the Royal cousin just needed some special attention and clearly wanted to be spoon-fed today. Physically the royal cousin was able to feed herself, so it may have been her emotional needs that required attention that day. I found it difficult to find any emotional needs being met.

Rachael was a feared member of staff who held a high opinion of herself and did not think so highly of others, and even I knew this was never going to end well for Lorraine. I've watched as patients have run and hidden the best they could on hearing her approach. I was convinced that they could recognise the sound of her footsteps on the hard floor tiles. As Lorraine returned to the cutlery drawer to get the Royal cousin a spoon, Rachael abruptly walked back to the dinner table with a look of conviction and picked up the plate of food with the intension of throwing it away. Lorraine snatched for the plate from Rachael's hands, but instead they were left embraced in a tug of war over the Royal cousin's food, as peas and carrots flew across the dinner table.

As the gravy from the plate splashed over Rachael's hand, I could see her losing her grip as the plate slipped from her grasp. Rachael clearly felt undermined, so she slammed the dirty plates in her other hand onto the table with an almighty crash, which I bet could be heard in every corner of the asylum, splashing food onto the walls and even onto some of the other patients, who were sitting there frightened and shell-shocked by the events unfolding in front of them.

Rachael stormed towards where I was sat, and where the other members of staff were sitting with front-row seats to the unfolding action, enjoying the confrontation that would soon be asylum gossip. Lorraine just ignored the gaggle of witches around their cauldron and, instead of continuing the battle, took the food left on the meal plate after the altercation to the Royal cousin. Lorraine began to spoon-feed her while giving her some calming words to defuse the tension from the eruption that had just happened. After some softly spoken words of encouragement to eat her meal, the Royal cousin complied, but I could still hear Rachael near me ranting to the other staff. She was complaining that Lorraine was nothing but a troublemaker and labelled her a liability who would cause complications. Surprisingly the other staff agreed with Rachael, one of them saying that Lorraine didn't fit in and wouldn't last long at the asylum. The others nodded in agreement.

I could sense the danger that Lorraine had placed herself in, as I knew that at the asylum words spread like wildfire. Lorraine could hear the other staff talking about her but not exactly what they were saying. She chose to ignore them and continue to feed the Royal cousin, which in turn only provoked the other staff more as they saw it as overperforming. I watched in awe as Lorraine fed the Royal cousin until her food plate was completely empty. You could see Lorraine's face gleaming at the sight of the spotless plate. Then with her rebellious persona and a defiant glint in her eye she stood back up and returned to the food trolley, and like a proud mother after an excellent parent evening, she collected the Royal cousin's dessert. She sat back down with the dessert and fed her the entire bowl.

She didn't stop there; instead she allowed and encouraged the Royal cousin to lick the bowl clean in front of everyone, with the same sense of accomplishment on her face as somebody who had just knocked back a pint of lager in one giant lug. I could see that it was not only Lorraine who was ecstatic about her personal achievement, as the Royal cousin was also overwhelmed by the one-on-one attention she was receiving.

After it was all done, Lorraine busied herself, enabling her to keep herself to herself and far away from the cold atmosphere as it slowly spread across the ward like the first cold snap of a mini ice age. It was obvious that Lorraine felt isolated, being given the cold shoulder by the other staff. As time went on the isolation put Lorraine into a cocoon-like state and fractured the care she could offer. To me it was saddening to watch her kind and loving act making her the target of ridicule and persecution. She was made to feel bad about the situation, just because she interrupted the ward's routine and stubborn, set-in-stone ways of doing things, even though I myself saw these stone tablets often re-chiselled, as routines and atmospheres would change depending on which staff worked the shift.

I could not believe that I was watching royalty living this regular life of terror and humiliation. To me there was nothing royal about her life – in fact it was barely even humane. Even when she was clean it did not seem to be for long' she was rarely fully dressed and lived in fear of the staff and other patients. You could see that many staff were both verbally and physically rougher with her than with others, and I suspected this was because of her lack of mobility. Being unable to verbally communicate also contributed to much of the abuse, as she was not able to defend herself or even shout for help.

However, I would hear her screams and moans – the meaning of which were pretty clear to even a child. Not only was she suffering neglect due to the asylum being understaffed, she was also suffering due to some staff being lazier than others. Some staff would just hide in the office in the wards in an attempt to avoid work altogether.

The basic needs of love and care that we all desire were lost in the asylum. I would often find Tinky on the floor, having fallen from her bed or her chair, and unable to get up without support, but staff were busy on other tasks or were not around. There were times she would fall in one of the corridors and stay there until some passing nurse or someone from the office came across her. She always seemed to be covered in bruises, cuts and even black eyes – an unusual sight to see on a member of the Royal Family. Her life was full of dangers and she was surrounded by volatile people, so most of the time you were not aware of where, how or when the injuries happened. You would not know whether her bruising and marks came from a fall, a volatile patient or the rough actions of certain members of staff. What I did notice was that she would flinch and back away from certain people, and you could see that she was living in fear and terror of something.

I would often think about the respect and honour the Royal cousin would have been given if circumstances had been different. The bathroom areas were private and seemed to be the areas in which I would regularly hear her screams of discomfort. As I was only able to hear and not see what was happening, I put the screams and slapping sounds down to her discomfort with the situation; I was soon to discover something far more sinister. Even from the beginning, it was pretty clear to me that her slowness and confusion in the mornings would irritate certain staff. Unusually, her needs were regularly met by the male staff, who would bathe and dress her, and change her pads. It just depended on who was working that day.

There were not enough staff to meet the toilet needs of all the patients regularly, so pads had to act as nappies. I would notice that these pads would be so heavy and pulled her clothing out of shape where they had not been changed for a long time, even sometimes for most of the day. I could not imagine the discomfort she must have been in, and as the day went on I imagine the discomfort would have increased. It would make me happy when I would see her dressed in something I had bought for her, but most often I would see another patient wearing the clothes I gave to her.

The system at the asylum was that after the clothes had been worn once, they would go to the laundry rooms – where those patients who were able would work. More often than not, the clothes would then be lost in the system and did not go back to the same ward.

Not a great deal of attention was paid to making her look nice and respectable when it came to anything more than washing her. It was a shame because I would moisturise and massage her hands, which she loved. The only times I saw her with make-up on, people would laugh and mock her. They made her look silly, like Minnie Mouse.

Many patients' clothes would be removed as quickly as they had been put on, and they would wander the corridors undressed or half dressed. You would often see these individuals being manhandled and marched back to the wards, being pulled around as if they were rag dolls with no dignity. I would regularly see naked men and ladies and got used to it, as clothes weren't ever brought to them, or blankets, as would happen in the world beyond the walls; they would just be guided, or dragged, back to their wards to be dealt with. It seemed that everyone who entered the asylum had a spell cast over them to ignore the obvious and to accept the nonsensical.

Breakfast consisted of the full works, if you could call as much aeroplane-like food as you could eat a treat. There was a lot of screaming and shouting around the breakfast table – most of it coming from the staff, who had to manage twenty to thirty hungry patients, all of different abilities. Sometimes, under supervision, I would be allowed to help spoon-feed some of them. The Royal cousin would need help at times, and I loved to support her as it was a very sensual time for us, like when a mother bird feeds her chicks. The Royal cousin needed me and I could feel it by her tight squeezes of my hand while I put food in her mouth. Staff would be rushed at meal times and often seemed to forget that these individuals were not machines. The Royal cousin would stuff her food down in fear of losing it to another patient, as food would be stolen straight from her plate or even mouth if left unguarded, or if her attention wandered.

All the wards would finish breakfast at similar times, and the corridors would begin to come alive with movement, as patients would be left to attend one of the three day centres depending upon their needs. The Royal cousin was at liberty within the grounds to wander freely, meeting friends from other parts of the hospital on her way, greeted by both staff and patients as they passed her, which would usually be acknowledged by one of her grunts. As well as walking the corridors, she would go in and out of the two large fire door entrances to Kaleidoscope, a day centre that was set up like an adult's nursery. There was a stage with a large dance floor, and this is where I would see the 'spinning man', who would be brought in each morning by staff and left to lie in the middle of the wood-tiled dance floor. Here he would spin a silver lid from one of the kitchen pots, or if he did not have this I would watch him remove his trainer and spin that on his finger with ease.

There was a television area with chairs around it, but the strong smell of urine that became more pungent as you got closer to them would put anyone off from sitting on them. There were also tables and chairs set out where patients were encouraged to do some colouring or painting, and they were often found cutting pictures from magazines. It was the same routine Monday to Friday, and had been so for as long as I could remember. At the weekend when the day centres were mainly closed, there were just the corridors and passing faces to amuse her. The neglect and loneliness was so very obvious.

There was nothing wrong with the Royal cousin's senses; the moment she heard the noise of the food trollies and smelt the food she would make her way back to the ward, consumed by the thought of lunch followed by pudding. The puddings were lovely; I would often share some extra jam roly-poly with her if it was on the menu. 'Curtsy,' some of the staff would say to her before giving her anything to eat or drink. She would awkwardly bend her knees and tip her head, then slowly straighten her legs back to receive her pudding or cup of tea. The arch in her back made these movements seem both awkward and painful, but they were required for the release of whatever it was they had.

After the lunchtime madness came the same process as in the morning. The doors of the day centres would reopen, and the residents would join those patients who came in from the community and were fed in the centre. The Royal cousin would spend much of the afternoon doing the same as she did in the morning; her day was very repetitive, as was much of her weeks, months, years and decades. At four o'clock, the day centres would close for patients to have their evening meal back on the wards. Depending on who was on duty, she would either be fed slowly with care and affection, or be forced to curtsy before receiving her food, and then fed without care and in haste. There seemed to be no continuity of care; it really would depend who was working the shift, and whether other patients were playing up and monopolising their time. I watched her being force-fed on many occasions.

My father would do the same thing with me at home when there was a meal I didn't like, so I could understand her misery and embarrassment with every mouthful. I would hide the food under the corners of our dining room carpet when Father was not in the room, to return later and discard them in the bin or feed them to the dog. The Royal cousin did not have this option and at times would be forced to eat what she was clearly disliking.

The asylum entertainment did not end there, because even though it would seem that the staff car parks were empty and the majority of staff had gone home, the day centre Kaleidoscope, unlike the other day centres, would open its doors again for some evening entertainment. It wasn't until about eight o'clock when the doors of Kaleidoscope closed that the Royal cousin and others were left with nothing but their own entertainment.

When it became dark outside and there were fewer staff around inside, the atmosphere and energy seemed to change, walking around the asylum in the artificial light. The Royal cousin would walk or sit on the cold floors of the corridors with no real purpose, her life seemingly empty and incomplete. The interaction she would have would be when she was cornered by another patient, or struck while being passed by others. You could hear her regular moans for peace. Unlike me, she was not able to hide beyond the heavy fire doors, using them to slow the pursuit or move quickly to escape a patient's grasp. I don't think they wanted to hurt me when they chased me, but being alone and trapped with one of these patients when they were being over-friendly was just as scary as being around the violent ones.

Many doors were used to contain patients; they were locked at times even when they should not have been. I would often see patients through the long, skinny glass windows in the fire doors, the banging echoing through the corridors – there would always seem to be someone somewhere banging against one of these barricades. Even though it was safer for the Royal cousin to stay on the ward, she loved being untethered and embraced it, whatever the dangers. Keeping notes and learning all that I could about my friend, I was starting to get under Mother's feet, and when around staff who were from outside, I was very often encouraged to 'go play'. One day a member of staff working with Mother told me to 'go and guard the royal tunnels'.

Chapter 9
The Royal Tunnels

One morning I awoke to screams of terror and our family dog yapping and snarling downstairs, as if somebody had let the postman into the house with a bag of doggy-licious letters and parcels. I quickly drew back the curtains and peered through the window to see a beautiful morning and the tranquil sun glaring down on our home. However, breaking the peaceful scene were some frantic movements across our back lawn. All of a sudden it looked as if a stick of dynamite had exploded in my garden. A bevy of doves had been feeding on our lawn, but at the sound they immediately shot up into the clouds in wild array. Their stunning white feathers falling back to the grass looked like somebody had shaken a snow globe. I was barely awake and very confused to see that the rabbit run had been pushed over on its side, releasing the rabbits and tortoise into the garden to run freely.

It would normally take Speedy the tortoise all day to cross the width of the lawn, but I had never seen him running as fast as he did that day, kicking his little legs behind him as he crossed the garden in record time. It was making me feel dizzy to watch both of our goats, tethered to a post with rope, vigorously spinning around in circles like a washing machine on spin mode. The garden was lit up with excitement; it was like watching a faulty David Attenborough wildlife documentary stuck on fast forward. I saw Father's strawberry plants divide like Moses parting the Red Sea, only for my rabbits to appear and then immediately disappear under the goats' shed.

They had clearly given up on foraging through Father's vegetable patch in exchange for somewhere to hide. Suddenly, the metal stake that was tethering the spinning goats pulled from the ground, releasing them from their imprisonment. They ran round to the front of the house and disappeared out of sight. After opening the bedroom window to see where the goats had run off to, I could hear Father's bellowing voice coming from the side of the house. My attention was immediately drawn to all the cooing from the flock of pigeons on the roof tiles overhead, and then to the branches of the enormous trees surrounding our garden. The high-pitched squawks coming from the obviously distressed crows, lined up all across the branches, was ear-piercing. It sounded eerie and looked weird and satanic, like the spawn of Lucifer had just been reborn among the long grass of our back garden. Suddenly from the side of the house both of the goats returned, running with their untethered ropes still attached to their collars.

More shockingly, about two seconds after the goats came flying past, Father appeared running at an equal pace but with a petrified look on his face that would make babies cry. Then unexpectedly, charging after him one second later, came two enormous and vicious Alsatians, gnarling and snapping at Father's heels with saliva dripping from their huge, sharp teeth. Charging forward and in mid-pace, I watched him reach for the ground – he seemed to just collect a handful of grass. After he repeated this for a second time, luckily in his grasp and tightly gripped in his hand was one of the loose ropes attached to one of the goats.

He tugged on it tightly and pulled the goat towards the back of the house, before they all disappeared. A split second later he reappeared but without the goat. He instantly and without hesitation or thought for his own safety headed out heroically towards the hectic and aggressive dogs, who were chasing the other terrified goat. The goat was running for his life, the snarling, blood-thirsty dogs taking chunks of flesh from its body.

Before jumping into action the last thing I saw was my father trying to reach the goat while running around the garden dodging gnarling dog bites, like Pac-Man darting around his maze avoiding ghosts. My whole world was coming crashing down around me. Our home was under attack. To those ferociously hungry dogs my home was like Burger King or some kind of multicultural restaurant with delicacies from all around the animal kingdom. Our garden was going to be turned into a slaughterhouse and I was about to witness an animal massacre. At that moment I wasn't sure if the Royal Family had sent their bloodhounds or attack dogs to permanently silence their inhumane secrets, or whether this was just payback for my goat having previously attacked a member of their honourable family.

I ran downstairs barefooted and still in my pyjamas to discover the multicoloured budgerigars chirping manically and wildly flying in circles around their cage. Our tiny West Highland White Terrier was no match for the ferocious dogs that were violently attacking us. He just continued to bark and whine in fear in the corner of the room. I entered our kitchen to thankfully find the goat that Father had just saved bleating crazily in our kitchen. He was clearly distressed and was covered in bites, and his fur was glistening red with his own blood. Mother was screaming frantic instructions to Father through the open kitchen window. With the acrobatics of a circus performer, Father grabbed and swept up the rope attached to the goat that remained in the firing line of the two monstrous dogs and pulled him towards Mother's instructing voice.

One of the dogs took a swipe at the goat and remained attached to the goat's rear all the way to the back door, which Mother had opened. He stayed attached to our beloved pet until the moment she saved Father and the goat from an unthinkable fate by slamming the back door onto the dog, which released its grip to let out an almighty whelp. After Mother closed the back door, I looked out of the window that she had been shouting through to see the other dog violently toss a rock with his nose, flipping it through the air before it landed back on the grass with a loud thud. As I looked I realised in horror that this was not a rock but Speedy, our tortoise, who had sensibly taken refuge in his shell as the monster dog gnashed at it.

As I watched in horror, I was hardly aware of a voice in the distance screaming, 'Rocky, Bozo, come home now.' The dogs began to bark even more frantically and scratched at the bottom of the goat's shed, where the rabbits had burrowed to hide. The shouting became louder and I realised that the dog's owner was coming up our driveway to retrieve his monstrous animals, but before they could be snatched away the dogs had one last attack left in them. This final battle was almost biblical, a modern-day David and Goliath. With no place to go, Speedy stood his ground on the battlefield to protect our home and family and avenge the injustices against the goats and rabbits in a battle with the two vicious attackers. Speedy stood his ground and placed himself into a defensive position similar to a large stagnant rock. He was just about to launch a devastating attack and release a whole world of pain upon the two unexpecting victims, when suddenly the dogs must have smelt their owner. The snarling Alsatians instantly stopped mauling Speedy and after some more barking darted off in the direction of their owner as if nothing had happened.

After the coast was clear and free of danger, Father ran to his car and pulled the rear seats down. He then came and picked up the goats, one under each arm but so gently they hardly made a noise, and took them to the car. Luckily Mother had already covered the goats in towels to protect the car seats from all the blood, and we all got into the vehicle. Father sped off so fast that you could smell the tyre rubber in the air. As we sped out of the driveway, I thought I saw a shadowy character standing behind an electricity pole next to the fence of the house where the dogs had come from. I just caught a flash, but he looked very familiar.

It was lucky we got the goats to the surgery so quickly, the vet told Father. The next day, unfortunately only one of the goats came home alive. I spoilt that goat so much that day; anything it wanted it got to eat.

The detective in me wanted to know how the dogs had escaped from their caged garden, which was just a few doors away from our house. They had lived there for as long as I could remember and they had never got out of their restraints before. My mind kept going back to that half-hidden figure. Where had I seen him, or it, before?

I would often walk past the garden with the dogs and think how their caged life compared to the cages that the volatile predators at the asylum were kept behind. That kept niggling at something at the back of my mind. I had wanted to free those patients, but look what the dogs did when they were freed. What happened to the patient I met, the one that did get away? Was he the shadow I saw?

It was because of the close locality of the vicious creatures that I had to continue to ensure that the goat was safe and would never have to endure or experience anything like that again. I decided to keep the goat by my side as much as possible. He and I ended up spending more and more time together and our connection and bond grew. I walked him even more than I did the dog. It was the royal goat who had survived, so I guess that after time had healed his wounds he was probably feeling a little bit humbled by the whole experience. He had chased royalty through the asylum, and now he also knew the feeling that the Queen's cousin must have felt when she was running for her life from him.

It had made sense to me that the tunnels that I had played around hundreds of times with my goat were named the royal tunnels because their entrance was in the middle of the front lawn of Royal Earlswood, or even because they were said to tunnel underneath the main building. However, I was to learn that the name had a much more exciting and interesting meaning. The two arched entranceways would become symbolic of who I was becoming, and this would be the place where I could always remember who the Royal cousin really was, an acknowledgement of her royalty and the one place, made in stone, that shows her once royal connection.

I was told the first of the many stories that I would go on to hear throughout the years about the tunnels, but this was the most exciting time for me as it was the very first. I was only nine years old, and perhaps not of an age where grown-ups should have been filling my head with such tales, but in the asylum I was often treated like an equal by the staff, or was just not noticed when these tales were being told. From the stories I heard, these were the tunnels used by members of the

Royal Family to visit the Royal cousin in the past, long ago. I could not believe it – why had I not been told this before? It seemed that the secrecy of these tunnels was as important and unspoken as the royal resident herself.

Lips were definitely looser on the subject when it came to talking about some old tunnels than talking about a member of the Royal Family, and I began to have an insight and even deeper understanding of her life. I ran to the tunnels instantly, and with their new alluring enigma, I intended to walk straight into the unguarded, unsealed entrance to take in the dark piece of history – a history that was secret to the outside world.

The first time I heard the story, I ran out of the main building, across the quiet private drive and down the embankment, and there it was. As I got to the entrance, closer than I had ever been to it before – thanks to my father's horror stories – I peered around the open doorway. As I looked I could see some steps going down deeper underground but no further, as it was so dark. It was scary for me to just look into the tunnels, and I did not feel comfortable; there was a very eerie atmosphere and I could only imagine the worst – that there may be rats and dead bodies down there.

You would have thought that the first thing I would have done was get a torch and go back, but I was so scared and did not want this ceremonial place to be ruined by what I might see. I was very intrigued at discovering that members of the Royal Family had actually been there using the tunnels as a private passage to their relative. To think that they had once gone to so much trouble to guarantee access to their loved one. It was also clear to me that they had not been used in a very long time. It answered a few questions in my head but opened up the doors for many more.

There was nobody who seemed to know much about the tunnels that I was comfortable asking. All anyone could tell me was that they were used to access the Royal cousin many years ago. They now lay in ruins, probably with only rats inhabiting them. The big question for me was where they led to. Most people were in agreement that they went all the way to Earlswood train station; some staff even said they reached back several miles to Redhill train station. Either way it was a secret route for the Royal Family to come and visit the secret that they had been keeping; it also showed the lengths they would go to in order to keep this existence at the asylum top secret. Knowing the lengths that the royals had possibly taken in the past when they might have visited added a whole new level to the secrecy of the lie that I was now a part of.

I felt like a spy with information that only a selected few had access to. It heightened the level of importance and secrecy my role in her life had taken. Seeing the tunnels in the ruins in which they lay showed how she had been forgotten as time had passed. The cousin's royal life lay in ruins just a short walk away from where I stood next to physical ruins.

The goat walks with Father increased and I would always choose the route directly to the field where the tunnel entrance lay. Father was even less brave than I was. I think all the stories he had been telling me had somehow warped his own mind and convinced him not to enter the tunnels at any cost. He would poke his head under the arch as I did, only to quickly pull out while trying to keep his macho image. If you were to hold out your hand beyond the entrance you could barely see it as it was so dark; all you could see were several steps taking you deeper underground and then you could just see some rubble and the tunnels seemed to disappear around a corner. There was no way of seeing where these tunnels led to and no way that I could convince anyone to go down there. Even the patients would not go into the secret passageways as they were so dark and frightening.

I made the decision that it would probably be better if I were to guard the entrance to the tunnels from the outside, not from within. My information was limited to begin with, but I was amazed with this entrance – it was as if it was from another world. I didn't know if it was a direct route to Buckingham Palace, but I hoped so. I would spend hours on the grass just beside the dark entrance with part of me expecting a group of guards followed by members of the Royal Family to pop out. It was the secret entrance to a real-life fairy tale, and I had a place where I could reflect on all that I knew. It felt like I had the proof of her royal existence and the connection to her royal blood and heritage.

The arches were proof to me of the true link she had to our British Royal Family. Paperwork it seemed could be altered or destroyed, but the cold stone and stories of this place would confirm all that I was learning and knew of my royal friend. We could only share these moments when the weather was fine, as it was only during summer fetes or spring fairs that the Royal cousin ventured out onto the front lawns just next to the royal tunnels. I believe the Royal cousin would have enjoyed walking the grounds more than she did, but it seemed that the only escape from the asylum building was when she would catch one of the large, heavy fire doors opened. I would often see her waiting for another patient to open them, as they were far too heavy for her.

I would imagine the tunnels like another blueprint in my mind, but I could not picture where the other entrance would be. I would walk with father searching the fields and land near the train station, but the secret entrance eluded me. I guess that if we did not have a goat with us we might have looked strange searching through the fields, but our pets were the perfect cover for searching grasslands and bushes freely. I tried to look up information in the library about the tunnels, only to find what seemed to me to be false facts about these passageways. These claimed that they were used to deliver coal, and there was nothing that made any sense to me. Surely if the tunnels were there for the delivery of coal from the railways, then the size of the entrance holes would have been larger, but instead they were only big enough to walk through. If the tunnels were for deliveries you would also expect them to be closer to where other deliveries came to the asylum, not right at the front of the main grand entrance with only steep steps or a sharp hill to the asylum. None of this made any sense and seemed clearly part of the catalogue of deceit.

The only thing I found out at the library was where the other entrance might be – which was Earlswood train station. This became the centre of my searches from that day onwards.

If I were to uncover this piece of the puzzle on a Sunday afternoon while sitting around on the ward, then what more could I discover if I were to step up my game, adding a little more pressure for the answers to all my questions. Maybe I was asking the wrong people? The information on my royal friend was stacking up and my hunger for more became greater, but I was never expecting to hear what I would soon uncover.

Chapter 10
Alone

The royal tunnels seemed to be the perfect starting point to begin conversations about the Queen's cousin. People seemed to love to talk about the mysteries of the tunnels and the secrets that they held. I would see excitement in their faces as they talked with amazement about the royal link to the asylum. It was as if they didn't think they were breaking confidentiality if it was the building and its history that were the objects of the conversation – the royal link being a mere detail.

To me the rat-infested ruins of the tunnels symbolised her misfitting, dirty, torn clothing, so she stood almost equivalent to the ruins – equally forgotten. It was an abusive and disrespectful way to treat another human being, even if you forgot about her being a royal. Her lack of power had been exploited by those in power – even within her own family. It seemed to me they would do whatever it took to keep their power and authority. I always wondered if every member of the Royal Family felt the same about their secret, or whether they were just following strict rules, their own code, and had lines that could not be crossed. I even questioned whose side I was fighting for. I was not sure whether I was working with the Royal Family – like being on a secret mission – or whether I was alone with my feelings and the Royal cousin who had been left to find her own way like the ruins of the royal tunnels.

Through my Christian upbringing, I learnt from a very young age that I should care for those less fortunate than myself. I was sure that the Royals must have the same beliefs as I did as I watched the TV coverage of all the religious ceremonies the family attended and how they behaved when at church. I was just hoping they would act on one of the basic principles of Christianity. The fact that they did nothing to make sure that their Royal cousin was well cared for and safe made me wonder if these shows of Christian devotion were just pantomime for the people, without any real personal meaning. Surely to admit a mistake and fix the problem would be a more royal solution than just remaining in ignorance about what was being done. The amount it would cost to rectify their lie would be insignificant compared with the costs of just one royal event. I was often shocked to see the display of wealth while a member of their family was clearly troubled. Not all the abuse she was inflicted with was behind closed doors; it was there to be seen by anyone. The suffering did not appear to even touch her family, but it was affecting me, and if they had just learnt about her distress then I was sure they would intervene.

It was hard to watch with my own eyes, and I could not believe that the Royal Family I was brought up to trust and believe in would do nothing to change it. It made no sense and showed a brutal side to the monarchy that I had not believed existed. The brutality of leaving a Royal in the asylum was the sort of story you would hear or read about in histories of the kings and queens of the past. Stories of cruelty and the fight for power had resurfaced and were very real to me.

I lived in fear for her as she was already meant to be dead, so half the work was already done. This behaviour, by the secret society, could surely not continue in a time when the world was becoming so politically correct. I had seen how much work members of the Royal Family do when it comes to charitable causes, however the actions I was witness to were contradicting all that was on show. Was I one of the few who witnessed the Royal Family's real feelings towards the disabled? The Queen's cousin's existence was a secret and there was nothing I could do to change that – except writing the letter that I did. I knew something would have to change, as it could not just be ignored.

The long-term side effects of the daily, passive abuse were not clear, but it was obvious that the neglect she was subjected to was having a direct influence on her behaviour. I would sit in the corridor and observe her walking up and down the long, stone walkway without purpose. I would watch her as she struggled, even in pain at times, as she was never assisted nor had any form of walking aid. She would flinch at both staff and patients and be weary of interactions.

The violence and distress she was witness to, or a victim of, were regular and abundant. She was around distressed patients who were often locked behind doors, and regular outbursts of anger were inevitable. She was often in the wrong place at the wrong time and would be caught up in it, helpless and scared. I would frequently see patients held down by multiple members of staff while one would inject the patient with something to calm him or her down. There would often be distressed or naked patients running through the corridors. The Queen's cousin did not live peacefully but in fear and distress. Everyone she ever knew had neglected her. Rejection and neglect in her daily routine, and rejection and neglect from her family, the people who could change this with just one letter.

It was clear to me that the Royal cousin was not at the asylum for her safety as she was at more risk of violence and injury than she would be anywhere else. Her personal care was not a priority and the amount of quality time staff spent with each individual patient was minimal. Some days she resembled a tramp or somebody who had just barely escaped an explosion. There was clearly not any financial or emotional support from her family.

I found that having the support of your family was a necessity within an asylum if you wanted to be protected from the most horrific sights and events. I witnessed things that would make a man out of any small boy. I grew up fast because it was impossible for Mother to protect my innocence by shielding my eyes from all the sights and sideshows that the asylum had to offer. Please don't think for a second that my childhood was lost or stolen within those asylum walls, because it was only expanded – expanded beyond dreams and even fairy tales. It just meant that walking into corridors or wards of naked adults became a part of life. I learnt to look away or close my eyes tightly while Mother tried her utmost to hide all the penises and vaginas from me, but this was an asylum and they were on show everywhere. Sometimes even closing my eyes wasn't enough protection from the sights of the asylum. To my horror and disgust I have been face-to-face with naked patients who had painted their clothes back on themselves by using faeces extracted from their own bottoms, head to toe. In each and every one of these cases, running seemed like the only legit option for me.

There were too many disgusting sights and stories to remember, but some I would never forget. Such horrific stories as patients removing their own eyeballs from their sockets and then leaving the eyeballs rolling across a ward floor were a struggle for me to believe were possible – well, that was until the day when I walked into Mother's ward to discover a biology lesson that I never wished to learn or be any part of. I immediately had to place both of my hands over my nose and mouth to cover any air holes from the disgustingly pungent fumes that were being released.

I'm not at all sure which internal organs were laid out on the floor in front of me by a patient who was continuously pulling more from his bottom, but I was haunted by some of these sights as I walked through the creepy asylum. Then there were the stories about the patients who bite body parts off other patients. Any body part that stuck out, like a finger, toe or even a penis was a target. Thank goodness I never witnessed a severed penis, but I saw various blood-soaked hands with parts of fingers dangling in the wind.

I would always try to have my eyes to the floor scouring the ward or corridor while I sang my song out loud, to the amusement of the staff. I may have laughed, but while other children at schools were singing songs regarding 'heads, shoulders, knees and toes, knees and toes', I was walking the asylum singing 'fingers, toes, eyeballs and penises, eyeballs and penises' praying that I wouldn't stumble across any of these savagely pulled or bitten off body parts. I would have never considered myself a chart-topping singer and songwriter, well, not until the day that I entered a ward to hear the words to my song being howled out by a member of staff and accompanied by a chorus of patients. My song was clearly taking off, with the added bonus of newly introduced dance moves that would put the Macarena to shame. I don't like to blow my own trumpet, but there is no doubt in my mind that I wrote and introduced the number one asylum hit, and I even had royalty shaking her bum and partaking in obscene dance moves to my 'Eyeballs and Penises' song.

Questioning staff about the tunnels, I would ask the question why, only to hear stories of bloodlines and cover-ups. I was often told, from what seemed to be a genuine source, that the only possible reason for the lack of support, secrecy and complete collapse in communication was because of a shameful secret. However, the way I saw it, there was no reason for the Royal cousin to be left helpless without any support or contact. I was told there could be a darker reason for the denial and lack of communications with her. The talk within the walls led me to believe that there was a more sinister reason for her to be written off as dead, that she was the result of an accident and that the Royal Family were trying to keep their bloodline pure. The stories were hard to believe but told frequently.

Could the need to keep a Royal bloodline white and noble result in the secrets I had discovered? I had already seen the consequences of the lies so was fully aware of the power they held. I became aware that we could not trust these people in power, with all this greed and corruption overpowering their love for their own family. It seemed to me that they felt no compassion. It felt as if the Royal Family clearly did not care and was just good at hiding the truth. If I had not seen it with my own eyes I would have never believed it. As the world around them evolved, I could not believe she was still left there for dead.

This home of the Royal Family was also residence to perverts, sexual predators, and was even a place where prostitution was accepted. The asylum had a prison mentality with the black market currency of the institution being tobacco. Many patients did not even wish to smoke it; instead they would chew or swallow whole the cigarettes with the desperation of a heroin addict in need of a fix. You would see some patients constantly searching ashtrays and floors for dirty cigarette butts to smoke or eat to get the nicotine hit. Staff would encourage it and use the currency of cigarettes to make patients do things they would not usually do – or ever want to do. Sometimes the promise of nicotine was used to relax violent episodes or to calm aggressive patients, without the realisation that it just encourages future aggression.

This nicotine addiction produced an accepted market for prostitution within the asylum. The need and desire for the drug was much greater than that you would see in the outside world, and with much less control over their unmanaged addiction. Patients would take advantage of one another, having their bodies raped or molested for simple gratification in exchange for the drug. These needs of the patients managed to ruin my school trip to the local farm; I was too embarrassed to ever look a cow in the eyes again. I had been informed by a member of the asylum's staff that patients often escaped to make love to a cow in a field. Now at that age I wasn't too sure what making love to a cow entailed, but I was pretty sure there would be a lot of cow kissing involved. I became so much more protective of my goat. I ended up urging my father to lock the goat's shed at night with the key rather than just shutting it tightly. I did not understand what the poor and lonely cow must have suffered on those beastly nights in a grassy field under the moonlight, but I was damn sure that I did not want anybody romancing my goat while I slept.

My Royal friend's birthdays and Christmases were both a joyful and upsetting time for me. The neglect and loneliness seemed to be amplified by the celebrations and decorations that were everywhere. After I discovered her true identity, she did not seem to fit in with the hustle and bustle of the asylum. She would seem so lonely and alien to her habitat. Each year at Christmas, I would listen to the Queen's speech hoping – half expecting – that she would send a message or even send well wishes to all her family, which would then start the process of change. However, each year I would find myself disappointed. It was as if the letter I had sent had been ignored.

Some staff would make the Royal cousin perform as you would a dog. 'Curtsy to your family,' they would say whenever the royals appeared on television. It would really anger me how disrespectful some staff would be towards her. Most of the time it wasn't even said in a nasty way; it was just entertainment to them. She would not recognise anyone on the television, but they would act as if she did – even mocking her at times. With any televised royal occasion I noticed that she would become a sideshow and attract much unwanted attention.

The Queen's cousin's Christmas and birthday gifts never consisted of anything significant. She received nothing of any value and mostly all she got was received by her with gratitude. I would always check the tunnels on these occasions, hoping and wishing to spot a sign or any movement, but they would remain in darkness. The life she should have been having beyond the grounds of the asylum was taken from her; she was a prisoner of sorts. It seemed that her only real luxury was food. The ample food and drink at parties would make her happy, even though she would be denied the freedom of having what she wanted when she wanted it.

The Royal cousin missed out on so many royal occasions, but surely it was never too late to correct the mistake? As each passing royal televised event would make no mention of my friend, I would feel both anger and sadness. It seemed the amount of charitable work done by the Royals would mount up, but no support for the Royal cousin ever came. It was as if the media-driven charity work that they did was just for show. I truly believed that one day the Royal Family would welcome their relative back into their lives and make good on their mistakes, but instead they just continued with their lavish existence while she lived her life of suffering all alone.

I was sad one Christmas Eve and could not get the royal cousin out of my mind. The thought of her waking up again on Christmas Day in a cold asylum conflicted with my own happy Christmas Day ahead. I went to the asylum to see the patients as I always did around this time, as it was a very exciting and happy time for them. With the televised celebrations turned up loud on the ward, I suddenly felt so sad that she was alone. To comfort me in my obvious distress, I was told a story that the narrator had thought I had heard before, but it was definitely the first time I had heard this mind-bending, chilling, Christmas piece of information. I was comforted by a member of staff with a warm hug and the unmistakable smell of mince pie on her breath. It was then, with what she meant as comforting words, that she said, 'She's not alone.'

Everything I thought I knew was about to change again.

Chapter 11
Not Alone

I could completely understand what the asylum's Royal Family were suffering, but did anybody really comprehend my own heartache?

That cold Christmas, when I was feeling at my lowest, I was briefly lifted by a few simple words from a member of staff giving me the idea that someone had finally come for the Royal cousin. It wasn't the cold air that evening that was giving me the chills, but the thought of my royal friend being taken away from her living nightmare and the web of deceit. I was happy at the thought she was going to a new life. However, just a few sentences later, I was to discover that I had never been so wrong; it was actually the opposite of what I had understood, but still a comforting thought for the short term.

The happy faces of the patients and the tinsel, placed randomly around the walls, must have blinded me, but she very innocently told me that Tinky was not the only royal at the asylum. That there were other members of the family there. This talkative staff member told me how the Royal cousin was lucky, especially at Christmas, to be here with her relatives when the majority of the other residents did not have that privilege.

Once again, I jumped to my own conclusions. As I could not see the Royal cousin in the hall full of patients in Christmas hats, I was sure that she was having a private family moment somewhere top secret and away from prying eyes. Probably in one of the lavish rooms by the front hall that gave the illusion that visitors were somewhere very different from where they actually were.

I was not expecting to hear what was then explained to me. As my questions poured out about the Royal Family's Christmas reunion, she corrected me. 'No, she is not being visited, don't be silly. There are three other members of the Royal Family already living here, a male and two females who are also patients.'

I replied slowly in disbelief, 'OH MY GOD!'

The relaxed atmosphere around the Christmas celebrations had seemed to loosen tongues more than usual. She even told me the locations of these new royal figures within the asylum, and I could not believe my ears when she informed me where some of the female royals were situated – as they had been right under my nose all along. It felt like I had been here before and I wondered if this rollercoaster would ever end. It seemed that I was riding the rollercoaster in a carriage that only possessed three wheels, as the next words uttered from her mouth shook the entire fairground. 'There was another female,' she said.

My jaw dropped so low it felt like it needed to be picked up by hand from the floor before I could process and question what this woman had just so innocently told me.

'Where is she now?' I asked, pleading with her, using my sad eyes as a tool to find the whole truth.

She told me about a Royal cousin who had died. She went

on to reveal the upsetting news that Tinky, the most mobile Royal cousin, had a sister who had also lived at the asylum but had passed away very recently. As Mother regularly took me to a multitude of different wards and introduced me to the majority of the staff and patients at the asylum, I knew that I would have known her. I instantly felt robbed, knowing that under my watch a secret had slipped past me. I felt deceived and tricked by the unfairness of not knowing her true identity or her importance in our history books. I was not the only one being robbed of an important icon in my life, as her passing had robbed her of a companion and the true friend that she would have found in me, The Royal Guard. The member of staff informed me of another secret cousin to the Queen who was at the asylum but died even before I was born.

Walking back to the ward, my brain was working overtime. Could this all be true? Was the Royal cousin really not alone in this asylum? I had so many questions as I pushed open the large, heavy door of the ward Mother worked in while mumbling about what I had heard.

I could hardly finish my last sentence before being shushed by Mother, but in the background somebody else laughed and said aloud, 'Yeah, but they are meant to be dead too.' That solidified it for me; all that I had been told was true and the secret I was a part of became six times larger and only fuelled my passion to guard these royal individuals, as I had been taught as a boy scout 'to do my duty to God and to the Queen.' The knowledge that the Royal cousin was not alone would be temporarily pleasing to me, but also seemed to open Pandora's box after the initial surprise had passed.

'I play with dead members of royalty,' I told myself. This was an unusual, but very true, fact that I had to keep a secret as a child; it sounded like something you would hear in a horror movie. Maybe if I only knew this information it would have been easier to deal with, but talking and interacting with those who were meant to be dead was hard for me to get my head around. At the first opportunity to speak privately with Mother, I asked her if I had ever known or been in contact with the asylum's royal who had recently passed away. Mother confirmed my suspicions; I did have a relationship with the deceased royal.

With this news my gut began to do somersaults, as did my brain to this new-found information. I now realised that this Royal cousin had been deprived not only of her identity and true royal heritage, just as the one who died long ago had, but she had been deprived of The Royal Guard – the one and only person who would have treated her with the utmost respect and honour, putting her on a pedestal and respectfully acknowledging her as the true royal she was meant to have been. I could not understand how the law would allow and assist in this conspiracy, and could continue to keep these lies, which were directly affecting four people's lives. Surely faking deaths would be fraud or another criminal offence because of the implications regarding birthrights – especially for people of great importance.

I could not understand how the leader of our country and her relatives could allow such a death sentence to be placed on their own family. How could they deny them any knowledge of the world beyond the asylum walls? I could not believe that this could continue in the society in which we lived. I was sure that change would be just around the corner. Sometimes you really should be careful what you wish for.

There were now six secrets, and four dead royals, sharing my kingdom. Who was to say that I would not at any moment bump into a couple of princesses on my rounds at the asylum? From what I could gather, they had all been in the asylum for most of their lives. I wanted to give them all glimpses of the outside world, sharing with them some of what they had been denied. Two of the newly discovered Royal cousins were completely accessible to me as they were on the same ward as Mother's patients – three if you included the one who wandered the corridors and popped in and out of the ward to interact with Mother. One of them was bedbound and hidden away in a private room in a quieter area of the ward. The other was more mobile but hidden under a false name, Choppy. With Mother working on her own in the evenings and throughout the night, as part of the night-time skeleton workforce, I could easily spend time and share moments with them.

I needed to know. I wanted to see with my own eyes whether this male cousin really existed. To no prevail, over and over I begged Mother to take me to meet the male royal. Mother resisted, even though she could see the sadness in my eyes and disappointment in my face. This was not an easy task for her to fix as the logistics for me to enter the hospital block were far from simple, unlike all the unlocked wards.

On the down-low, without Mother's knowledge, I intended to look to see whether or not his throat held a surgical scar like Tinky's did. I couldn't ask Mother or get her help as she was very sensitive about the whole subject of royal throat slashing. No, this was something I had to do alone. To be honest I had to discover whether all the asylum's throat-slashing horror stories were true. I had to see with my own eyes whether the cold surgical blade had been used across the throats of royalty more than the once that I had already discovered.

With two of the Royal cousins already being underground, having died twice, the evidence was lost forever, and I would be left to wonder whether they had both been physically silenced to hide the Royal Family's secrets. I made it my mission to find the truth before any more evidence slipped from my grasp. I wasn't going to make any mistakes. I was going to be as surgical as the blades that may have passed their throats. I had to individually check the Royal cousins myself for the voice box removal scars. When I found myself alone with the cousins, I pretended I was sorting the collars on their clothes and took a good look at their necks and found no evidence – well, that was until I physically lifted their chins. Then fear overtook every cell in my body as I saw the surgical scars. At last I realised that the chilling rumours were true.

One day out of the blue and to my absolute surprise, Mother called me over to her office saying that she had something extremely important to tell me. My face wouldn't stop glowing as she told me it had been arranged. That was going to be the day that I would meet the secret, registered as dead, male member of the Royal Family. I was overjoyed at the thought of Mother taking me into the hospital block but was quickly disappointed that Mother had to call in help for this secret mission. Mother explained how one of her trusted colleagues would be taking me because herself, or me for that matter, had no reason to enter the hospital block, and she feared that it might raise some eyebrows if discovered.

I didn't have to wait long before my guide arrived to take me to detect my holy grail. I couldn't contain my enthusiasm and you could see I was bursting with excitement as it was the final piece of this puzzle – and yet another part of the huge royal conspiracy. Before leaving, my guide turned to promise Mother that I would be kept very safe. I was already aware of the route we would take because in my mind I had imprinted the secret location of the last royal like a pirate's treasure map marked with a huge X to mark the spot. I could see the many gruesome stories told in blood on the brickwork as I followed my guide through the menacing corridors. I didn't know it at the time but soon this anecdotal brickwork would be splattered with my own blood and eternally imprinted with my very own royal tale.

I could feel my stomach begin to flutter and as we approached 'cockroach alley' nearing our destination, the butterflies that I was feeling in my stomach began to spin like a sheepdog chasing its tail. I glanced through the last remaining window of the corridor to see the deserted grounds. At the time I did not know that this would be the place where the royal assassin would soon arrive to destroy the secrets forever.

I took the final nervous steps down the sinister dark windowless corridor until we came to the heavy door that opened up onto more evidence of the royal conspiracy. There was a huge pause as we stared vacantly at each other when my new friend asked the now terrifying question, 'Are you ready?'

I replied with a simple 'yep' as I was unable to form a whole sentence. I was so nervous and felt really shaken. Nerves controlled my words as if I was its hand puppet. She pushed open the heavy door to my treasure island. At the time I didn't truly understand the importance of this intense moment that I was about to have. This member of the Royal Family would be the only one who would never be discovered.

I am changing the history books just telling this story – so pay attention.

The heavy door was opened up to see yet another door, now locked inside a broom cupboard with a window looking into the hospital block. After opening the secondary door, I was introduced to a ward of lined up beds, and to my surprise the room was unstaffed. After the Royal cousin's bed was pointed out to me, I immediately ran the gauntlet as quickly as my legs could manage, scooting around a table and darting around chairs like a mouse running through a maze heading straight for the block of cheese in record time. I manoeuvred myself around his bed until I was face to face with the Royal cousin. I reached across his body then quickly and without thought of any consequences I tugged the hair on the top of his head, pulling off a full rubber face mask and revealing his true identity. The unmasked imposter angrily growled the words, 'If it wasn't for that pesky kid we would have got away with it.' Beneath the mask I revealed the Queen of England, mastermind to the whole evil conspiracy.

No. Stop. Wait, that was a Scooby Doo cartoon that I'm thinking of and I definitely didn't own a giant, talking dog, as I had a goat for a sidekick.

To be honest I should have been at home watching cartoons instead of living a life that was a reflection of one. My life had all the characteristics of a full-length animated *Scooby Doo* cartoon, and I was unmasking conspiracies on most days at the asylum while in equally haunting destinations as in the animated series.

Like the characters in the cartoon, I too was that pesky kid who was prepared to go to any lengths to prevent the villains of my story getting away with it.

What actually happened was that when we reached the heavy door to the hospital block, we stood at that solid door in great anticipation of a slick and smooth unannounced entrance into the unit, softly floating in like two leaves gently falling in autumn from a great oak tree. The mission I was on was nowhere near as simple as I led people around me to believe. For me this was going to be a double mission; not only was I planning on uncovering yet another allegedly already dead member of the Royal Family, but I was also there to discover whether or not he had also had his voice box removed to ensure the royal secrets remained hidden. I cringed so much that it hurt my cheekbones as an enormous creaking sound was released as the second door into the hospital block was pushed open, the echoing sound alerting everybody in the quiet room to our unannounced arrival. The element of surprise was immediately lost. It was as if we had triggered off a bank's security alarm system.

The two members of staff who were patrolling the hospital block immediately stopped what they were doing, and I felt their scorching eyes staring at me as if I'd been dressed in a bright-orange prison jumpsuit to highlight my every move. As they stared at me with their piercing eyes I could see that they were questioning why I was there, so I just awkwardly smiled back. Before our noisy entrance, you could have heard a pin drop within the secure unit. Without any patients there wandering aimlessly, it was a far cry from the hustle and bustle of every other ward I had seen. As soon as those two members of staff laid their eyes on me I knew that the stopwatch had started and I only had a limited time before my presence in the unit aroused questions, and it would not be long before I would have to confess the real reason and that I knew all about the royal secrets held in the asylum. My guide went to have a short conversation with the two members of staff, leaving me standing awkwardly in the centre of the room. Before she left me she secretly signalled with her pointed finger and whispered, 'That's him.'

As I stood there alone it didn't matter from which angle I slyly stared at him – I was unable to see whether or not he had the surgical scar on his throat. The secret royal gentleman stared back at me with a vacant glare as if he was just existing, but I was still massively humbled by the historical moment we were sharing alone. I had no doubt that yet another dirty royal secret and the asylum's most hidden and protected crown jewel existed. The thought of ripping off the Royal cousin's bed sheet to reveal the throat-slashing scar passed through my mind over and over, but instead I stood there like a lost meerkat until my guide returned to collect me and escort me from the unit.

As I left the unit, the two members of staff continued to stare directly at me; it was as if they already knew my true reason for being there but they didn't dare say it out loud. After the two doors to the hospital block closed behind us I forgot about my shyness as I could barely hold my excitement as we walked the sinister corridors back to Mother's ward. As we made our way back, the kind guide asked me if I was happy and whether I had got what I had come for. I couldn't exactly tell her 'no' because I was unable to see whether he possessed the telltale throat scar, so instead I lied and said, 'Yes, thank you so much, I got everything I wanted.'

She returned me to Mother and we could both tell from the looks on each other's faces how happy we were. She clearly knew how very important it was to me, and she was ecstatic that she had managed to fulfil my deepest dreams and desires.

I was talking freely about the royal conspiracy with a multitude of staff within the asylum, yet every question answered only raised even more. I had seen with my own eyes that pure evil was at work within the asylum, so however strong that need was for answers, fear kept me tactical and my feet grounded. I enjoyed all the conversations I had and even learnt to enjoy my own voice, which meant that having discovered that vital body organs could be removed to protect royal secrets, I became protective of my own voice box. I was learning at a young age the capabilities and reach of the Royal Family as well as what they are prepared to do to protect their lies. Like a cat burglar in the dead of night with a hand as steady as a master safecracker, I prowled the asylum in stealth mode going from patient to patient, bed to bed, throat to throat whenever it was possible and I was alone with any residents.

I spent days, weeks, months, and eventually years moving

shirts or blouse collars and lifting dribbling chins searching for scars. Instead, I found no evidence in the entire asylum that the barbaric deed had ever been suffered by anybody other than the asylum's monarchy. It was definitely unusual that the royalty had these throat scars, which seemed to back up the stories, but what I found more unusual was that nobody else in the entire asylum did.

The abandoned Royal cousins became my extended family and were as important to me as my immediate family. Each had their own personality and it was hard not to fall in love with them. The bedbound female member of my new family had very limited mobility, so I would read to her, play musical instruments, or just spend time around her bed letting her know she was loved and not alone. Just talking to her and showing kindness would please and entertain her. The entertainment I provided was neither grand nor lavish, or what you would expect for royalty, but it felt good inside knowing that I was doing something.

Seeing the royals lying in their beds, under bare hospital sheets and with cold, hard, metal bed frames, seemed so far from the lives that had been taken from them. The complete lack of possessions always made me sad, and the way they were neglected, not even allowed family photos to visually stimulate them, was also upsetting. I also know that two of the female Royals at the asylum had been given different names. I didn't know whether the names Tinky and Choppy were part of the cover-up or were given to them by disrespectful members of staff. To me it seemed an extraordinary coincidence that the only two royals who were still mobile had both been given false names, while the bedbound royals retained their own identities.

The bedbound female royal had to be fed using a spoon. I was allowed to help feed her at times – a sensual moment we would share. The solitary life she had without visits or changes in scenery did not seem fair treatment for even an animal. The neglect was once again so obvious, and her sentence was equally cruel.

A request for a rise in my pocket money so that I could clothe these royals properly was rejected by Father. The thought of me now buying clothes for four members of royalty, rather than one, was too much for my father to comprehend. I wasn't sure if he first heard about their existence from my lips, or whether he had already been aware of them and was a member of the secret society that knew everything. I was not tied down by fear or by the threat of losing a job or a pension as everyone else seemed to be, but I was still terrified of the retributions for my handwritten letter to the Queen.

The thought of all the Royal cousins living on only hospital food was insufferable, so I would often force Mother to bake scones and teacakes at home, as well as make cucumber sandwiches with the crusts cut off. I would then pack them all in a biscuit tin ready to share with my royal friends. Each time I took china cups and saucers from our display unit at home to finish off the illusion that we were somewhere else other than within the asylum's haunting walls.

To my delight I would make this a regular occurrence and have my own royal tea parties at the asylum with real-life members of the Royal Family whenever I chose to, an experience that others could only ever dream of. The other patients on the ward would behave like packs of hungry wolves, smelling the delicacies from what seemed to them to be another universe. Although they had three hot meals each day, due to the lack of staff or lack of supervision mealtimes would become a battle for the food, a fight won by the stronger patients, leaving the weak hungry and battered. Maybe it's not as simple as a choice, to be caring and to commit kind acts towards others. Maybe other people's fortunes are already mapped out.

To me the persecution of these individuals in order for the family to keep its genetically pure royal cloak, covering up or erasing errors and any signs of weakness, was prehistoric. These individuals were being dismissed as a curse visited upon the Royal Family. It was as if there was an inner circle that allowed this torture. How could somebody be living in their home spending the inheritance of these discarded family members and still hold their head high and call themselves royalty? I could see no logic for what had once happened to them, but it seemed profound and cruel.

I had learnt about the Nazis at school, and sometimes I felt that the Royal Family must have some of that identity indented in them somehow. How else could one account for all the secrecy and their willingness, in fact preference, to send away their flesh and blood, when infants, to be treated in this unworthy way. In my eyes, those who knew and did nothing were as bad as, if not worse than, those who condemned the Royal cousins to living this life of poverty and abuse because they were considered biological threats to the Crown.

I was unable to understand the absolute poverty they were living in. Just knowing that one was there seemed unusual, as I would have thought her heritage and what she would have been heir to would have more than taken care of her medical and social needs, but now knowing there were four royals in the asylum made me think it strange they did not have their own care facility. They could certainly afford to pay for it. It felt like the lie about their deaths was both unfair and unlawful. Any property, land or income that they would have had as their birthright would have helped and changed their lives for the better. The thought that their financial support would have gone elsewhere when so desperately needed seemed scandalous. How could four royals be living in rags with torn bedding while others with equal birthrights swallow money up without guilt as if there were no end to it? I could not imagine the Royal Family wearing dead people's clothes. The members of staff which the Royal Family have at their beck and call would have been more than adequate to care for the Royal cousins. It would have made me proud to be British to see the Royal Family as part of a caring nation. I grew very fond of them, even before I knew the true extent of their decadence.

I am sure that the nation would have accepted them with open arms and not rejected them as their own family had. The basic need for love and for a real family should have stood head and shoulders above everything else.

I would wonder if the same results would apply to another member of the Royal Family if an illness did not surface until later on in their life, or if they were involved in an accident that would not be something that would be considered a biological threat. What are the boundaries and scale that the Royal Family use to identify their rejects? What if Prince Philip, the Duke of Edinburgh, or even the Queen had regrettably degenerated before their unfortunate deaths?

The Royal cousins' home would at times be more hazardous to their health and wellbeing than their illnesses. Everything that I took for granted on a regular basis was lost to them. I would often think of them with regular lives, having letters after their names and commanding the respect of everyone they crossed paths with. I could even imagine them at royal celebrations with their staff, family and friends.

For all this to happen just the once could in some twisted way be put down to a mistake, but for it to have happened multiple times proved to me that there was definitely a structured system, like when they would reject dented cans of beans at a Heinz factory. I did not know whether to believe they still had these beliefs or it was just one of those occasions where you lie once then have to keep lying to continue the original lie.

Even at such a young age, I felt the world changing around me and was sure that the shame of what they had done would overpower the shame that they felt over their disabled relatives. So many charitable and good things were happening in my everyday life, including Children in Need events and Red Nose Days, that it seemed that as a nation we now had a bond and sense of duty to these individuals less fortunate than ourselves. There was a sense of pride when helping a fellow human being. If I, a complete stranger and just a child, was able to form a bond and have a relationship with them, then so could their actual family. I wanted them to just fly away from the asylum, as did the white doves that migrated to and from my garden.

I was sure that change was just around the corner, but I would need to wait patiently for that day to arrive. Until then, I made it my duty to do my best for these presumed dead royal individuals. Little did I know but my most courageous test was just around the corner, as the day when a royal assassin would take aim at royalty was already approaching fast.

Chapter 12
Keeping Secrets

I had been blind for too long.

At the same time, day-to-day life became mentally complicated for a young child with so much information. I felt like I had a whole world of secret knowledge at my fingertips while the rest of the planet was left in the dark. I was keeping a secret – six secrets – for the Royal Family. These secrets seemed to be at a detrimental cost to the people involved. All I could do was continue to wait, hoping that my letter would reach Buckingham Palace. I asked God to help their poor lost souls while we waited for a response. I needed to watch over the remaining four the best I could until the day came when they would be taken home and accepted back into the family. I had a real gut feeling that day would come soon, as I could not see any way that the current poverty and neglect could carry on. I had no choice but to continue to keep the lies secret, and not to think about the consequences of it so much. However, the more I tried to not think about it the more it monopolised my every thought.

I was holding on to so many lies on so many different levels that I felt like I was giving myself a top-grade education in the art of spying and deception. On the one hand, I was keeping these royal secrets, secrets from the highest order, but on the other side of the coin I was in secret communication with the Queen – and, with these communications, I was risking it all. I knew that if Mother or anyone else was to discover my real desires before I posted the letter, I would have been banned from going to the asylum, or worse Mother would lose her position and our family an income. This did not stop me as the need to put things right overrode my desire for things to remain the same. I found myself writing more letters, to only soon after destroy them. It was as if it were my therapy to release the secrets I was holding in some way. It felt as if I were living a double life, as a spy would, keeping secrets for the Royal Family and continuing to preserve the offence. It felt as if being The Royal Guard consisted of a lot more than just the care and welfare of the secret royals; I also had to maintain this lie and betrayal for the Royal Family.

At the asylum I felt relaxed, like I was not keeping anything in and having to lie about who I was spending my time with, while in my academic life I was not able to divulge all I had done or who I had been with that morning, evening or weekend. Instead I kept uncomfortably silent with the excitement of personally knowing royalty – and dead royalty at that. To be honest, I enjoyed the double life I was living and the time I shared with the monarchy so much, and I felt that what I was doing was the honourable thing. I felt special, which was enough for me to keep going. I did not want to risk it all so I kept the secret, even during the difficult times when I most wanted to reveal it to teachers or friends at school.

At times it felt as if I were on a higher plain than everyone else, and at times even school came secondary to my loyalties to the Royal cousins. Having the knowledge I did, I felt myself above all the playground politics. I had truths, secrets and lies from the highest level above all others. I had my royal duties, and would amuse the three female Royal cousins by reading and providing fun activities. I would draw funny portraits for them – which they would hold and treasure for as long as they could before other patients took them away, as they did with most of their possessions.

Most people have to train for many years before being selected for their excellence to perform in front of royalty – not me. During those dark and murky nights at the asylum, I held my very own Royal Variety Performances. I would learn magic from books at the library and then gather props from home to perform at the asylum. After weeks of begging Father, he even subscribed me to a weekly magic comic, which gave me new tricks to perform. To be honest nearly all of the card tricks were too confusing and lost on them. There was this one time when to my astonishment I actually did make a sponge ball disappear, only to discover later, after searching the ward high and low, that it had been eaten by a patient who had been enjoying my show a little bit too much.

I knew that however good I became at magic that none of my magic tricks would ever compare to the wizardry that had already been performed on the Royal cousins by the able members of the Royal Family. You know, the illusion that had already made them disappear. My rubber chicken, disappearing balls and removable finger may have been considered basic magic by some, but the royal reaction was priceless. As well as mystifying them with my tricks it was always a joy to see them smiling, laughing and to be the cause of royal happiness in a place where you could film horror movies. There was also singing and dancing and there was a brass musical piece, introduced after I had been upgraded from playing the recorder at school. Because I was the tallest boy in my year I was given the largest instrument, which meant my proud parents got to listen to me playing the huge French horn whenever they wanted to – and even when they didn't want to.

The French horn's introduction to the asylum and my Royal Variety Performances didn't go so well because with one massive and intense blow of the brass mouthpiece when I was in the corridor, I managed to ignite the asylum and bring it alive with a mixture of high energy screams and cheers. Like the goat, the mighty French horn was banned, and that was the first and last time I was allowed to bring it into the asylum.

At times I had to bring the two lives I was living together. I would complete my homework while on the ward with the royals, which would always leave questions in my mind on whether what I was being taught was actually true. I was keeping one of our history's secrets, and I knew that our history books could be altered to suit the needs of the people in power.

Knowing that our history books could be altered, I found what I was taught during lessons questionable and I started doubting everything. I was confused over what information was completely believable, and would find myself questioning all that was put forward as fact. The idea that I would have to complete future exams on these false facts was daunting. The sacred facts, which are important to the whole world and future generations, being falsified would be a huge thing to admit to, and I started to believe that the powers out there might choose to remove the problem rather than embrace it. Deaths being fabricated would only leave people, just like I was, with many more questions and wondering about other conspiracies.

The treatment of my royal companions could also be compared with many of the horrific historical stories of the past, the treatment of the less abled, and actions of past royalty. Stories of The Mad King would echo in my thoughts, as kings locking children in towers and plotting deaths was a little too close to what I was witness to. If anything, I felt as if I were a 'knight in shining armour' coming to their rescue. I even imagined what their lives would be like if and when they were officially saved. I would imagine visiting them at their own home on their own land with staff caring for their every need.

Then there was also that other strange figure, the man I had met in the dark. Something told me he was also guarding them. On my walks in the grounds, I often felt eyes on me, especially when it was getting dark. I sometimes imagined that one day the two of us would swoop down on the enemies of our royal charges, and save them from the worse their family could do.

It was as if I had a sixth sense, and I felt I was able to see lies everywhere, as if I could sniff them out like a bear chasing a picnic basket. I felt as if the altering of our history books and Royal Family trees could just be the beginning, and it was opening my mind and the doors to other secrets.

At this stage I would believe any theory, no matter how outlandish. There were many sightings of aliens and UFOs that, however far-fetched they may have seemed, were still something I could not disregard as others would so easily. Assassinations of American presidents and the whereabouts of Elvis Presley also did not seem out of the question to me. I was becoming a conspiracy theorist. I was one of a handful of people who knew this secret, and yet I did not feel alone. The image of the man in the dark kept returning to me, the man who was also guarding these people. Guarding the royals? Or were there other secrets, ones so bad they had to be shut away in the sinister locked units. I would stay up late at night thinking why were these buildings out there, so far away from the main building?

I could not believe that I had stumbled upon the one and only time this kind of lie had been told. Having the ability to change lives and history books would be far too appealing to only use the once – well now at least six times. Six lies, which were then upheld by following generations, cannot have been the only ones. I was determined to sniff out any that I could.

I would regularly get on my knees and ask for help, but God was not answering my prayers. I was finding it difficult to keep my faith in something when I had no proof of its existence. Just having a book as proof for a whole way of life began to become less appealing to me, as I knew now just how paperwork could be altered to suit the needs of those in power. It felt wrong to be looking for errors and contradictions in the Bible when my family was so dedicated to the church, but I found myself unable to stop looking for conspiracies.

I went to Sunday school and spent hours at the church with our vicar. I would always question his faith, and the amazing stories he had read and quoted from the Bible each Sunday. Feeling secure that he could not pass on any information that I told him under God's rules, I nearly told him several times of my worries and the double life I was living. He would always make me feel comfortable, and I was able to speak freely. Yet, I would always stop myself just before the words left my mouth because of my constant fear of the repercussions on Mother and her job, and the fear that I would lose my contact with the Royal cousins whom I had grown up with.

It felt like everybody around me at the asylum had been rendered dumb and I, a child, was the only one who was capable of independent thoughts. Not only had I developed an extra sense for danger at the asylum, I began to actually feel the royals' pain and suffering. Even my nightmares escalated as I began to dream of police chalk lines around dead bodies coming to life. My thoughts would spiral as I added up all the pocket money I was owed by the Queen for the clothes that I had purchased for her living-dead family. This meant I was partly paying for the conspiracy.

While infiltrating the Royal Family, what was I turning into with all the cover-ups, secret societies and silenced witnesses? I wasn't going deeper into the rabbit hole, I was the rabbit hole itself, and I was constantly burrowing deeper and deeper. I was being pulled into the corruption within the Royal Family at a very young age. A conspiracy that shaped and dictated my life, meaning I formed my own belief system built from experience instead of textbooks. Once you have seen the world with these eyes and from my perspective there is no going back. Who knew which way it would go; I could either become a hero or a villain.

I was becoming older in my mind than I was in my body, and I found myself disinterested in childish discussions. Who fancied whom in the playground was of no interest to me as I was preoccupied with my own, grown-up thoughts and problems. Not being able to share the information I had with school friends and playmates made me feel as though I was lying to them as well. I had signed no agreement nor was I being held down by the threat of losing my pension, so I was under no obligation to keep quiet. I still knew inside I had to, and this made me feel very segregated and alone in my thoughts. I wanted to share my kingdom and knowledge with somebody so much but knew that hiding this lie was beyond my needs, so I kept my silence.

Chapter 13
The Royal Assassin

I was sure that one day the royal tunnels would once again come alive with the movement of royalty. I was not sure whether to expect a full marching band or the subtle footsteps of guarded royalty, but I was sure that something was on the horizon.

I would spend as much time as I could in the grounds. Most of the time I was given cola and crisp money to use in the social club or the asylum's patients' tiny tuck shop, and was pretty much left to wander freely. Children were always welcome at the social club, which was only a few seconds away from the royal tunnels. There were discos and live bands; in fact it seemed like there was always something happening at the social club for families, but I would always find myself wanting to be close to the tunnels, where I felt the real history of the royals and the asylum lay. It was so peaceful, as if I were the only one who knew or even showed interest in the royal tunnels. I was always alone there, and it became my special place. The only time I was aware of other people near them, or when I saw movement at the tunnels, was during the grand events that the asylum would host for the patients. This included an explosive event when I would have to take a bullet for the Royal Family.

The asylum would hold large events, welcoming the public into the grounds, even though it did seem as if it was mainly staff and their families that came. The patients would love any form of interaction with people without an illness – it was as if they had an illness radar that they would use to home in and make a connection with anyone able-bodied who they could touch. The resemblance that one of the asylum royals had to the Queen made it difficult to understand how openly they flaunted her in public. She had her fake and childish name, Tinky, as a cover, but I was sure that the regular curtsies the staff forced her to perform to thank them for food or refreshment, like a well-trained dog, was sure to give her away at social events. The other Royal cousins rarely attended these events due to their health and mobility, so it was easier to contain that part of the secret.

The sense of touch was very important to the patients; where all other communication had left them, it enabled them to remain connected. The happiest I ever saw the Royal cousin was on the days she was able to publicly celebrate her life and she was not locked away like a dirty secret.

The traditional summer fete and bonfire night seemed to grab the attention of local residents. The beautiful grounds would host the most stunning events, and the grass would swell with patients and the public integrated as one. The events that the Royal cousin attended were very grand and it was obvious that a lot of work and preparation had gone into them. Each year they would have a similar theme, and patients loved to dress for the occasion – usually in some form of handmade costume and headwear made for them from the rubbish and plastic found around the asylum.

There would definitely be no lobster and champagne at

the events, or any luxuries you would expect to see at a party with a royal presence. Nevertheless, the Royal cousin would be in her element, enjoying the constant flow of hot dogs, cups of tomato soup and fizzy pop. The simple prizes at the tombola and other stalls would please the patients, with their personal possessions being so limited. I would always win something for my royal friend and she would hold on to it for as long as she could, before it was taken from her by another patient.

However, I would always have one eye on the tunnels. I would see the public walking close to the entrance of the tunnels, and part of me would feel territorial and protective over my sacred place. It was clear that nobody else had the same awareness of the tunnels as I did. The way they would pass, giving only the briefest of glances, showing no interest of their royal history was a clear indication of this. If only people had been made aware of what I knew about the royal tunnels and the Royal cousins, this would be a place of national and international interest, a place where historical events had happened.

In front of the archways was my exclusive place where I could reflect upon all that I knew. It was somewhere I felt my connection to the British Royal Family the strongest, and if they were to ever come back using this route, I wanted to be the one to greet them first. My imagination would run wild, and I wished for a grand entrance by the Royal Family, or even just a floral tribute and message brought by palace staff. Though with each and every visit to the tunnels I would only be disappointed, as they clearly stood unused.

Not all the patients were able to join the celebrations due to their illness, mobility or behaviour. There would often not be enough staff to control all the patients at these public events, so many would be kept on the wards and away from public view. These patients would still get to attend parties, as occasions organised purely for the patients would happen throughout the year. I was lucky enough to be invited to many of these parties and would see the asylum alive with celebration. Like turning on a light bulb, the residents seemed to take over the asylum by their sheer numbers and excitement as patients and staff would relax and let go of their restraints.

The excitement of the patients within the walls of the asylum could hardly be contained around Christmas. A visit from one of the members of staff dressed as Father Christmas handing out presents was actually the happiest I ever saw the residents, as they were allowed to let loose and go crazy like school children locked in a sweet shop. I would watch Tinky being overwhelmed by the noise and the uncontrolled, overexcited patients charging around. It was clear that she would have preferred a quieter and more tranquil Christmas but was unable to escape.

The patients seemed to thrive on any occasion that consisted of dressing up or parading themselves in an organised clutter. Many loved to be on show and applauded, or really to be shown appreciation in any form and from anybody.

Although Tinky often looked very happy when dressed inappropriately and wearing handmade, silly costumes and hats, I knew that she and the other patients were only looking for the acceptance and the attention they rarely received. After decades of her living at the asylum, it sometimes seemed that certain members of staff had forgotten who Tinky really was, and which family she had been born into. At times it seemed like a who-can-dress-the-patient-the-silliest competition between staff, as the patients would parade in bin liners and cardboard boxes.

To see a royal in such attire was upsetting, but laughing at the patients was the norm for some staff. To see her forced into centre stage by her guardians and their antics, while people watched her, seemed an unusual way of keeping her existence a secret. I also felt anger as people laughed at her, the unwilling participant giving up any option to not participate in the sideshow.

I remember one day I was walking past her ward when I heard lots of laughter, which was such an oddity in the asylum that I wanted to see what was so funny. The sight that greeted me made me want to weep. Tinky was dressed in plastic bags, tied together with leftover Christmas ribbon and a plastic potty on her head, as if it were a crown, with some of the nastiest nurses gathered around her making her dance for their amusement.

'Stop it,' I shouted, making my way through the gathered ring of staff and patients, standing between them and their royal toy.

'Oh, don't be such a baby,' Joseph, one of the staff that was particularly cruel, shouted at me, and he tried to drag me out of the way. 'Go cry to Mummy,' he mocked me.

'I'll go higher than that,' I said in tears, 'I will tell the Queen when she comes for her family and she will put you in prison in the tower.'

'You think the Queen cares?' Joseph snarled back. 'You think they cut her throat because they care?'

'She doesn't know you people did that, and when she finds out she will make you all pay,' I said with my heart thumping so hard I thought it was about to explode.

'Who do you think put them here, boy?' I had no answer. 'No one cares about these poor souls, and we are just giving them a good time, aren't we, Tinky?' he said, turning to where she had been standing, a nasty grin distorting his face. 'Where the bollocks did she go?' he shouted at one of the nurses, as the royal was nowhere to be seen.

'Don't use that language in front of the boy,' the nurse insisted.

'We all have bigger problems than swearing in front of some stupid kid, where the hell did she go?'

No one had an answer and soon there was a mad rush, with selected staff searching high and low for the missing royal.

I was sure she had made a dash for freedom, that she had seen her royal guard stand up for her and remembered something about her royalty that had given her the strength to run. I was sure she was well on her way to the palace. I waited till everyone else was busy with the search in the asylum, and quickly dashed out of one of the heavy doors into the grounds and rushed to the tunnels – maybe I could catch a glimpse of her as she made her escape. By then, the siren was going and all the staff were alerted. It was November and the days were very short, so although it was afternoon it was pitch black outside. However, I was sure I could see two shadows moving quickly towards the tunnels. Had more than one royal made a dash for freedom?

Then I saw one of the figures fall and, before I knew what was happening, a group of asylum staff were pulling the figure up and dragging it back towards the asylum. I stood frozen with pain as I saw a weeping and screaming Tinky being dragged past me, her plastic-bag costume torn to shreds but her crown still firmly on her head.

I could not watch, and it appeared the search was over. So, who was the other shadow, I thought as I went inside. I gathered my schoolbooks and stuffed them in my rucksack, then made my way home, my face still wet with tears of pain and anger.

I didn't feel like doing much that evening, but I had an assignment to complete for the next day so I went into my room and dragged out my books as if they had been the offenders in the day's crimes. Then I noticed it, a red piece of paper tucked into one of my notebooks. I took it and unfolded the paper to see the words 'WE ALMOST DID IT, KID' written in big, black letters. I had a friend and ally, another royal guard, I thought, then suddenly the face of the man I had seen outside the hospital wing appeared to flash past my window. Was it him, was he there to help me, or was my childish imagination flying in all directions? I could not study and I could not sleep that night thinking how close we had come. Someone else felt as I did, I just knew it.

The incident showed me how low the Royal cousins had fallen. Their need for acceptance resulted in this willingness to be dressed as a pet poodle or as you would a small child attending a fancy dress party. When once I had loved it, I began to outgrow the childish entertainment of the asylum. It seemed that all the distractions and activities in the institution had the same theoretical idea, that these individuals should be cared for as if they were children.

The fifth of November, Bonfire Night, was a huge day at my home. It was Mother's birthday, and the entire clan would make a huge fuss over her. Our family would come from far and wide to spend that evening with us. Usually we would have a home-cooked buffet, birthday cake, and lots and lots of gifts. Mother would insist on us spending the occasion with all our family. This meant that each and every year we would all walk, or drive in two cars, to the asylum, where we would join the patients' biggest parade of the year. There would be fireworks, followed by a disco for the residents to enjoy.

Mother would insist on taking her birthday cake with us, and I would always make sure that we shared it with the Royal cousins. Guy Fawkes Night was a strange evening at the asylum; the loud fireworks and disco music would cover much of the screams and moans of the insane, and where it was dark you could hardly tell the difference between patients and staff. Only during the grand finale of glowing fireworks could I make out the faces of the inmates I knew so well. Many patients would want to meet and greet everybody attending the event and I would often look at other children with their scared faces gripping tightly to their parents, seemingly not as comfortable with the surroundings and occasional tight hugs from psychotic hospital cases as I was. People would walk by the Royal cousin without a fleeting glance, clearly unaware of whose presence they were in. I would wonder what would happen if they only knew all of the secrets I held close to my heart.

I hoped this day would have never come, but that day was the day I would look death in the face. The fireworks displays at the asylum were always nights to be remembered, but there had never been one quite like this before. Because it was also Mother's birthday celebration, I was allowed to wear my beautiful, brand new winter coat. I pushed my arms through the oversized sleeves and zipped it up just as we were leaving the front door. It was too big for me and so I complained to both my parents but they just said not to worry, I would soon grow into it. I was used to hearing this as it was standard protocol in my house to grow into your clothes. Father did the same; he would buy trousers that were too big for him and kept eating until he had grown into them. Just standard protocol. Anyway, that evening I did not mind too much about the oversized jacket because as soon as it was zipped up I began to feel an instant warmth as it took the chill out of the bitter cold November air. It was just Mother, Father and I attending the asylum; my brothers had another event and were meeting us afterwards back at home.

It was a dark night with just the neon glow from the

phenomenal exploding rockets in every direction above our heads, from different gardens across the town, to light the sky. I loved taking in deep breaths of the gunpowder fumes, which were everywhere. I was happy to see just a half moon smiling back at me as I looked up at the sky, for those full moons at the asylum still sent shivers down my spine. Unknown to me was the imminent danger that the Royal Family was in, and the full moon's antics were the least of my worries that night. After Mother had dropped off the birthday cake at her ward for the patients who could not come out, she re-joined us in the huge crowds of families and the asylum's residents who had gathered to make joyful memories.

Among the sounds of happy laughter and music in the air you could hear the crackling coming from the enormous bonfire, which polluted the atmosphere and was now all you could smell. The violent roaring flames of the inferno had embers hovering above it like flickering fireflies and the smoke stung my eyes and made my vision hazy. If the royal assassin's shot had been taken right then I doubt there would have been anything I could have done to save her.

Why after all these years they had sent someone to end their embarrassment, I will never really know, but having these unimaginable royal secrets in plain sight opened the door and gave the assassin an opportunity to make the hit and bury the secrets forever. What I didn't know was that the royal assassin already had the upper hand as he was preparing his mission long before I appeared, ready to strike without being detected by me or anyone present that night.

There was a good crowd and the assassin had planned well, waiting for the perfect moment to eliminate its prey. Then suddenly, without warning I realised that there was a commotion and I heard Mother say 'The patients have got out.' In that moment the realisation hit me that those patients kept indoors on such nights because they were too far gone had suddenly appeared in the grounds. There were shouts from the staff, some asking, 'Who opened the doors?' and 'The hospital block has been breached' while others were running around trying to gather up the escapees, thus making the crowd even bigger and more hectic. Of course, I still had no idea what was really going on, but I thought I caught a glimpse, once again, of my ally. There was mayhem, but little did we realise how lucky we were, as for the moment everybody was safe. Thankfully because of the crowds the royal assassin was trapped and boxed in, unable to get to the royal secrets and distinguish them forever.

Just before the display began, out of the shadows appeared the 'living dead' – one of the royals who didn't exist. Mother motioned Tinky and some of the other patients to come stand with us to watch the fireworks and join in with her birthday celebrations. We had a happy little group, and as the display began Mother quickly made me put my oversized floppy hood over my head for protection against the explosive pyrotechnics. The fireworks were spectacular and so loud that we couldn't hear each other speak. Looking back, it was the perfect setting for an assassination.

We watched Catherine wheels spinning like shrieking hamsters on jet-propelled hamster wheels until they met an undramatic end; then came the raging rockets that pierced the night sky like glowing ballerinas taking their last dance beneath the heavens before meeting their explosive finale. The light show was amazing, like a war of the worlds happening in the sky above us with planets colliding and galaxies exploding. I'm not sure what drew my eyes away from the light extravaganza, but when I looked down and into the distance I caught a glimpse of the long silver barrel of the weapon. I heard the pops, which left the gun smoking like a cottage chimney on a cold winter's eve. The next thing we knew, the royal assassin showed his ugly face directly in front of me and the crowds of people; all the spectators' expressions froze like deer caught in headlights. The happy and smiling faces transformed as their mouths dropped and eyes popped open as the royal assassin fell to the cold floor to take aim and shoot from the wet grass.

Everyone jumped at the same time as an almighty bang pierced our ears when the assassin fired again – then the chaos began. Instinctively Mother turned her body around, holding her arms out to shield the patients next to her. I copied her heroic actions to become a human shield protecting the secret member of the Royal Family, the target of the attack, I was sure, who was stood next to me. I had put myself firmly in the assassin's sights, but it was clear to me that I was going to have to take the hit for the team. I yelped as I felt a thud and then the hard impact seemed to vibrate down my spine; this was followed by a warm sensation as my back had taken the direct hit from the royal assassin's bullet.

Then came a perfect harmony of screams and terror from the onlookers, as if they knew their own fates if this explosive eruption of raging carnage continued. They had no doubt that it would be their turn next. There wasn't enough time for all of the audience to escape its fate as what followed was around ten seconds of hell on earth as the massacre began. It was like a buffalo stampede with men's, women's and children's faces lit up by the fireworks, but there were flashes of darkness after each massive explosion had burnt off its last granule of gunpowder. It sounded like popcorn cooking in the microwave – pop, pop, pop.

Mother and I were taking more body shots from the royal assassin, but somehow we both managed to hold ourselves up and stand our ground as human shields against the barrage of bullets. With my hand I reached around my body to feel where I had taken the impact. To my horror, I felt a large wet patch on my coat. I screamed aloud after I pulled back my hand and discovered it looked like it had been dipped in a tin of red paint. I looked at the ground and watched what looked like all ten pints of my blood leaving my body and dripping into the already wet grass.

The frantic screams of the victims unsettled the asylum's patients who copied the mayhem, completely unaware of the actual danger. Some of the patients were lambs to the slaughter as their immobility meant they had no chance to escape the barrage of bullets. It was a bloodbath and was pure torture to watch; blood was splattering everywhere. I saw what I thought were blood-drenched body parts whooshing through the air, but was relieved when I realised that it was just tomato soup from the polystyrene cups and frankfurters flying out of their buns. It was even a relief to discover that rather than blood, my new coat was also covered in hot tomato soup. Looking back, maybe that one rogue firework just didn't have the lift like all the others had, or maybe the sudden change in wind direction and the altered projectile's course was a test from God?

After the firework had dropped like a mortar and exploded into action by firing bullets of blinding light and glowing embers through the dark sky, you could see the look on everybody's faces when they saw that nobody had been burnt alive or even injured by the gunpowder-fuelled assassin firework, which had the precision, devastation and the unpredictability of a guided missile sent from Donald Trump to clean up this royal web of lies. It was a shame that the same could not be said about my once beautiful, new winter coat, which my father showed much more concern about than the possibility that my body was burning. Looking distressed,

Father shouted to me 'Drop and roll, drop and roll', expressed with such over-exaggeration and haste it was as if I had been doused in petrol and set alight. Mother shouted 'Calm down' to him as she patted down my coat and any hot bullets of embers with her hands.

Eventually we could all laugh about it when we saw that the danger had been averted. Well, everyone except for my father, who was still furious and even more mortified when I turned round to show him that along with the tomato soup stains were burn marks and holes in my previously pristine winter coat.

While some of the patients seemed as traumatised as our pets at home get by fireworks, the staff seemed happy that they weren't any injuries, thus saving them hours of work filling in incident forms. Other staff mocked the patients saying, 'They couldn't feel anything anyway', but I knew that wasn't the case. That night there wasn't going to be any need for yellow police chalk around dead members of the Royal Family because Mother and I had eliminated the threat to royalty. To be honest I didn't even know if it was an option for royalty to die for a second time.

I wanted a scar, but all I got was the immovable smell of burning in my hair to tell the tale that I was sworn to secrecy to never tell. I just had Mother to share my adventures with, so I looked at her with a huge grin on my face and said, 'I just took a bullet for the Royal Family.'

She couldn't hide her chuckling as she bent down to my ear and whispered, 'No, my silly child, you didn't just take a bullet, you took a missile for the Royal Family.' However, I just could not shake that feeling, the impression, that there had been danger lurking around us that night. Perhaps an innocent accident by a defective firework had averted a serious attempt to finally wipe out the secrets of a defective family. Had I really spotted an assassin, or was I just a child with a wild imagination? Had the other secret guard caused the distraction that made the assailant's mission a royal failure?

I could not imagine why suddenly they wanted their secrets completely wiped out. Why now? Was it my letter? No, that couldn't be, I convinced myself. The Queen would want to save her cousins, not remove them for good, that much I was sure of – then. I did know that I had to be single-minded in my mission and watch the Royal cousins and everything that went on at the asylum much more closely.

It was a very emotional but memorable time when I took that bullet for the Royal Family and I didn't believe that anything in life would ever peak that moment, but I never planned on committing the crime against the Royal Family that would make stealing their crown jewels look like child's play. It just happened.

Chapter 14
The Crime of the Century

I would see a lot of things happening on the grounds of the asylum when I walked or rode my bike there. As I watched the patients rambling freely, it seemed peaceful compared with the horrors that were going on inside. These horrors would speed up my daily, self-appointed training, quickly advancing me to the position I felt I needed to reach to help the Royal cousins. So far my letter had been ignored, and nobody was keeping a watchful eye over these abandoned members of the Royal Family. I could not understand it; they were disabled, OK, but what was so bad about that? Why did they have to be hidden and written out of history?

I was exactly where I was meant to be. I believed it to be my purpose and an important role, which had no precedence, and I would stand guard until they were safe and removed from this living hell.

Royal celebrations were always watched on the ward, with the volume on the large television turned up. The Royal cousins could not recognise or relate personally to anything that was happening, however they seemed to have an awareness of the celebration. Staff would encourage Tinky to curtsy to the Royals on the television, and she would obey on demand like a performing seal then wait for the reward, to the staff's amusement.

The cuts and bruises on her body, from falls or physical attacks, would haunt me. The lack of any explanation for these injuries only encouraged me to care for the Royal cousins' needs, and to watch over and protect them. I was witness to the distress they were going through but was not always there to see – and what I imagined was a lot worse.

Some of the most frightening and distressing incidents I witnessed as a child were patients having epileptic seizures in the corridors without support from the staff. I would often find a patient having a seizure while alone and have to run and find Mother or another nursing assistant to assist. This neglect would often be caused by the lack of staff, meaning that employees had little or no patient contact at times. Other staff would avoid patients who had particular needs by spending time in a locked office doing 'paperwork'. When there was a group of staff lacking the 'kindness gene' working together, the neglect was abundant. This would regularly happen as staff would plan and rearrange their own rotas so that friends, family, or staff of the same background and inclination would be working together.

There were numerous times when I would see patients held down by several members of staff. This would usually be followed by a calming injection of medication, rather than dealing with the patient's needs.

The manhandling of patients and violence had become a regular habit. Control and restraint techniques were implemented regularly as they were the easier and quicker option to deal with a patient in distress. Some staff would take pride in the control they had over certain individuals in the asylum. Being non-verbal and with very limited communication, I would worry as the Royal cousins could not report such abuse or attacks. These regular crimes against humanity were horrific, but did not compare in any way to the crime of the century that I was about to commit against the Royal Family.

Early one morning, I noticed that Tinky was reluctant to enter the shower room. It wasn't the first time I had seen this reluctance and obviously it was due to previous trauma. The tightly timed schedule to shower and bath meant that the less abled were regularly manhandled as they were rushed through this process. That day, Tinky protested by shouting and raising her hands in despair.

'Hurry up, stop messing about,' Maria, one of the support staff, shouted, waving her finger and pointing towards the shower room. Soon enough she was standing poised behind Tinky and began to push her. She then held her from behind, with arms wrapped around her body tightly, and dragged her in, feet trailing after her. As she disappeared, what was soon to follow changed everything for me. It was not the first time I had heard it, and it would not be the last, but this time there was something different about it and it was considerably louder than I had ever heard before. I could feel the malice as if it cut through the room like a Samurai sword.

The noise of the slap echoed from the shower room into the ward, followed by royal shrieks of pain. The slap was so loud it made me freeze on the spot, then cringe as I could feel the hurt and discomfort in the echoing sounds of terror. I felt so angry, but there was nothing I could do.

I heard the Royal cousin yelping clearly; it was her call for help. I had been witness to this behaviour before, but it was this incident, coming so close to the fearful events of the attempted assassination, that convinced me to act. It was that rock in the pool moment, the moment that started a catalyst of events leading to me having to enter the lion's den, risking my life and sacrificing everything. This day would lead to me having to forfeit something that meant everything to me. This day would lead to me officially becoming the royal guard, even though I had unknowingly been in training for this since I was born. It was as if I were no longer a product of random choice, but instead the universe had a purpose for me. That deep chilling sound would haunt me forever and put me on the path that would influence my own life and those of the Royal Family. The knowledge that I would gain would force more questions that would puzzle people much my senior, and begin the butterfly effect that would mould my existence and my beliefs.

You would have thought that the sexual allegations against staff or even the pregnancy of a patient would have been enough in itself to remove the royals from such a place. The worst abuse I was to witness, I was not yet even aware was abuse. I did not yet understand all that I saw.

Knowing the history of the tunnels, I was always discreetly aware of the Royal cousin's movements, and it made it feel like I was playing an important role in protecting them. I was fully aware of the secrecy involved, even though, within the asylum walls, it was talked about freely by staff and patients. Buying clothes from charity shops for the Royal Family gave me a sense of belonging and, in some weird childish way, rights over their destiny. All I could do was wait for a reply from the Queen. I knew that something would happen, as I had expressed my feelings that the Royal cousins could be targets, living in a minefield of dangers. I wondered for a while if I should send a second letter about my suspicions concerning an assassin, but then I realised I might alert the very people who were behind the attempt.

Shortly after the fireworks fiasco, my curiosity and need to act were overwhelming and I found myself pacing the lawn near the royal tunnel entrance with only my imagination to tell me what was beyond the portal. My training was over; they needed me. It must have taken over an hour to build up the courage just to decide whether or not I would attempt entering them again. I had tried several times before and only managed to get one foot in, but only with my eyes shut. This piece of our country's secret history was in plain view to the world, but only the few had the knowledge of its whereabouts. I was going to attempt to fulfil my destiny by walking in the footsteps of the Royal Family.

It was as dark as it could be, and there was a damp musty aroma as I neared the entrance. As I peered into the tunnels through the unsealed, pale stone arches, I decided it would be best to go head first for some reason. As I poked my head into the royal tunnels, while trying to tell myself this would be sufficient sacrifice to complete my initiation, the fear took over and I took five quick steps backwards so the asylum was in view again and I felt safe from anything that was living in the pitch black tunnels. After about one hundred deep breaths, with the thought of my royal friends who were in desperate need, I went for it again. My legs were still trembling from the first attempt and I buckled, finding myself even further from completing my task than the first time. Thinking about the possibility of there being something or someone down there was overpowering. I felt defeated and like I was never going to fulfil my destiny.

The next day was a Sunday and the sun was out, making it very bright, attributing to the day's feeling of positivity. Even though the tunnel entrance did not allow in any light, there was something about the sun in the clear sky that gave me a good feeling after a night of tossing and turning about what to do. It was as if the sun in the sky was my ally and made me feel very positive about what was ahead. It is definitely true what they say about the weather having an influence over your feelings; that morning it felt as if the bright and cheerful day would only aid me with the completion of my initiation. It was always very relaxed at the asylum over the weekends, and I just strolled straight through and out to the gardens without being challenged.

The sun lit up the front lawn like a golden parade awaiting my big entrance. I could not see the entranceway of the tunnels as I exited the main building, as it was underneath where I stood. I knew what I had to do, and that I had to do it then or might never make it. Standing above the tunnels unable to see the entrance may have made it easier to psych myself up for the few steps I had to take down into what looked and felt like the entrance to hell. I walked down the steps, which are actually the side wall of the entrance, which definitely helped as I could not see inside yet.

From the side and without even thinking about it, I approached the entranceway without a doubt in my mind that I would succeed in my mission. I did not want to give myself time to think about the process or to back out of the task as I had done on the previous day. I wanted to close my eyes and just walk straight in there, but my eyelids would not allow it for fear of not being fully aware of my escape route. With my eyes wide open, looking for any sign of inhabitants or other movement, I took my first steps into the tunnels and the place from which royal secrets had once emerged. I felt honoured to be standing somewhere that only a few people knew about, and even fewer had ever stood. I could not see a thing, but could sense the past being sealed down here. It was as if I were entering a tomb of the dead.

As I continued, taking the tiniest of steps, I was beginning to feel proud and aware that I had completed my task, and was now the unofficial royal guard. I didn't know it at the time, but this was also mentally preparing me for the crime I was about to commit. It was not enough – I was there, and I thought that I might find some royal treasure, maybe an old shield, sword, or even a gold broach similar to the one that my mum saw the asylum's ghost wearing. There and then, I made the decision to continue deeper into the tunnels.

It felt as if I were being watched from within the darkness – eyes were watching me. As I stepped forwards to collect my rewards of the forgotten royal treasures from years gone by, my dream was of finding a sword, but I would have been happy with a shield or some jewels.

Then it happened and it felt like the deep depths of hell had sent demons to block me.

Something flew straight at my head, and at the same time I felt movement on my trainer that sent chills through my entire body. For a moment I was frozen, unable to move a single limb. After what felt like a lifetime but was only really a second, too scared to turn my back on what had just happened to me, I ran backwards from the darkness and towards where I knew the light would be. As I reached the entrance, the relief that went through my body was like a force I had never felt before. It was overpowering. I did not think I was going to escape the tunnels. Nobody knew of my exact location, and they would not have believed for a second that I would have entered the sacred place, so I did not think they would search for me inside had I gone missing.

I lay down on the lawn facing the tunnels to contemplate what I had just done, and what had happened to me. I did not know what touched my foot, but I assumed it was a rat, and what hit me in the head I could only think was a small bird or a bat. I was just happy to be out in the daylight and free from whatever was in the tunnels. The collection of a rewarding sword or shield was quickly forgotten, as the sense of achievement was overwhelming. I had done what seemed to be the impossible, and I had finally committed myself to the honour of being The Royal Guard.

I was a cub scout and every Wednesday I would pledge my duty to God and to the Queen, wearing my uniform and saluting the Union Jack. To me, it meant something very different to what the rest of my cub scout group was swearing its duty to, as at each and every pledge to my Queen I would silently also swear my duty to the hidden and abused royals within the asylum.

It felt like the first day of a new life. I felt refreshed and ready for anything that was ahead of me. I was high on the achievement as a knight would have been, and was now anointed with my duty and sworn honour to the Queen and the forgotten, and supposed dead, royals, promising to guard them until they were safe.

I made my first duty as the unofficial Royal Guard to check on the Royal cousin who had previously suffered the consequences and trauma of the malevolence of a member of staff. I hunted the asylum until I found her – all alone. Now, I am far from perfect and if anyone thought I would get through my entire childhood without a few stupid moves then they would be mistaken. That day I must have been the craziest person in the entire asylum to do what I did, but I think I allowed my emotions to take over. If anyone ever found out what I ended up doing, I would have been banished from the asylum and put into a children's home.

Tinky was, as always, excited to see me, so I gave her a massive cuddle and took her hand to comfort her. I felt a dampness across my palm and I thought it was just her dribble, but when I looked down at my hand I was a little disgusted and shocked to see she had covered my skin with her blood. It wasn't like the other bloody scenes from around the asylum where blood is splashed around like it's a slaughterhouse, but it was still alarming to see. Quite quickly, I realised that she had been taking out her frustrations over her neglect by self-harming, and had been scratching the top of her hand until it bled. As I used the inside of my t-shirt to wipe her blood from my hand I had an insane idea. I know they say that you don't have to have the same blood to be family, but I wanted to clear up any doubt that she was mine. If the Royal cousins had been watched and protected as they should have been, then I would have neither made the choices I did, nor been in the situation where I did the unthinkable. Without thought of any consequence, I began to do something that made my nearly killing her with my goat previously seem minor.

The patients at the asylum were far from stupid; they were fully aware of the best place in the asylum to feel pain and self-harm to escape reality. I had witnessed many of the self-harmers use this spot for most of my life. The brickwork in the corridors where I was standing was the coarsest and harshest in the asylum. I was terrified of being caught, so I checked the corridor either way and kept my ears perked up for the sound of any doors opening. I began to scrape my finger along the edge of the corner of the stone windowsill until it bled. I had often run my fingers across the stained brickwork daydreaming of all the asylum stories they held; now with my splattering of blood I was joining the stains and history. To me the splodge of blood and new secret royal tale was art and held as much meaning as a piece by Banksy.

I didn't give a second thought to the risks of royal hepatitis or any other killer disease I might catch, as all I could think about was combining our DNA so our two families became one through the meshing of our blood. What I was about to do was like something straight out of a vampire movie, but I was somewhere much spookier than castle Dracula, having the asylum as my backdrop. I admit I was an obsessed little boy, brainwashed with the excitement of knowing members of royalty who didn't even exist for others. I didn't know at the time if stealing the blood of someone who didn't exist was even a crime. It wasn't quite a Viking blood ceremony as Mother had already banned any chance of us having a sacrificial goat at the asylum. I held my bleeding finger against Tinky's bleeding hand for several seconds allowing the blue blood to flow through my veins and mine through hers; in doing so I became her brother by blood and also joined the royal bloodline.

As I became a self-made member of the Royal Family it felt like it gave me a higher purpose, to be honest; from that day forward, I held my head a little higher knowing who my secret Royal sister was. After our blood was mixed, I looked her straight in the eyes and clearly said the words, 'You are my family now.' As I did, she looked back at me while giving me a broad smile – maybe for the first time she didn't feel alone, but felt included and wanted. That evening at home I could not stop thinking about what I had done and what I had risked to seal our bond, as she would now continue living through me even when she has left this world. I refused to wash her DNA off my hand; instead I allowed the royal blood to dry hard on my finger and it remained there for three days and three nights before I lost the final flake of regal blood.

I tossed and turned all night but could not get to sleep knowing what I had done. Instead, I lay awake tossing and turning until I could hear the morning birds chirping outside my bedroom window. Having earned my blue blood, I was now more royal than the future queens of England as even they will not have a merging of blood when they marry into the Royal Family. I wore my blue blood like a medal, but could never speak of the war I was fighting. Now if more proof was needed, then there it is, I just stole the blood of royalty – a child. What better evidence that the Royal Family was not safe at the asylum?

Chapter 15
Without a Whisper

You would never think it, but some nights at the asylum were peaceful and quiet; some even became a little uneventful for a child with adventure on his mind. When I say quiet I do not mean as peaceful as a library or a church during prayers, as there was always a constant moaning and howling, along with the occasional scream that would stop you from doing whatever you were doing and force your imagination to run wild and think of the possible terrors that would cause such a heart-wrenching shriek.

On such evenings, I would stroll through the grounds and walk the corridors checking for any hidden dangers and ensuring the safety of royalty in this spooky and dishonourable choice of a residence. It sounds unbelievable, a child acting as the only royal security in a place where there was danger around every corner and behind every door. What sounds even more crazy is that without that child's royal security there would have been absolutely nothing put in place to ensure the safety of our vulnerable and most secret royal history. Even these peaceful nights did not come without their own occasional surprises, and this was one of the reasons that I was taught by Mother to stay alert and to not ever let my guard down within the asylum.

On one particularly peaceful evening when my security rounds of the asylum had placed me on the top floor of the institution, I was alerted to a commotion on a distant ward. Further down the corridor the muffled shouting was so abrupt and intense that it could be heard through the thick wood of the fire door, which thankfully separated us. The hair on my arms stood to attention as I instantly anticipated the danger. I was very aware of my surroundings; being on the second floor, I was not in the best place to be trapped in the corridors with a volatile patient and without an external exit or an emergency escape route. The aggressive shouting became louder and more intense as it rippled down the corridor like a wave in the ocean until the sound wave broke against the corridor walls and ended up at my feet. I mopped the sweat from my brow as my hands also became clammy.

The aggressor's demands for coffee became even more frightening and I was afraid of what could be lurking behind the ward door. Often patients would travel from ward to ward demanding or begging for a hit of caffeine to quench their addiction, but tonight it sounded as if one of the residents was not getting the highly addictive caffeine hit that his body wanted and his addicted mind needed. Coffee withdrawal could be every bit as painful as booze delirium tremens, and a patient denied their 'drug' could become violent and dangerous.

'Aaaaarrrggghhhh,' I screamed out loud when my safety and security blanket disappeared before my eyes; I saw the large and heavy fire door fly open with an enormous crash as if it were going to leave its hinges and continue its flight through the air and beyond into the heavens. I was already petrified, then my skull vibrated as a ferocious and bellowing voice, no longer soundproofed by the enormous fire door, rumbled through my ear drums.

'I WANT MY COFFEE,' it screamed.

I could not see who or what yet, but SOMETHING extremely angry and terrifying was about to come through that doorway. Mother had prepared me for these exact unpredictable moments at the asylum. Nobody held a crystal ball and foretold the future so instead I had been taught the golden rule for any violent situation such as this: run. As I leapt into action and flew down the corridor, I wanted to look back over my shoulder to know what emergency I was running from, but as the shrieks for coffee became louder I knew that this had suddenly progressed and was turning into something beyond a search for a post-meal beverage. Before I reached the end of the corridor I heard another crash of a door followed once again by the psychotic demands for coffee; you could hear the urgency in the tone of the threatening requests until the dominant shouting was once again muffled as the door to the ward closed behind the caffeine predator.

After running to the end of the corridor, I stopped to catch my breath. I felt much safer standing near to the stairway. That feeling of security was stolen from me at the very moment that I saw the enormous monster for the first time. He had shoved open the ward door and appeared from within. His furious face was all screwed up and the colour of a ripe tomato; like an erupting volcano, he looked like he was about to explode. I was not shaking in fear due to the monstrous build and towering height of the colossus beast, or the screaming demands for an addictive substance that I did not hold, but as he stood before me and I looked him straight in his bloodshot eyes, it was who I recognised the screaming patient to be and the well-known warnings that came hand in hand with him that drove fear like a tsunami through every inch of my body.

The asylum was home to many amazing super-humans who I loved to observe as they performed their mind-blowing tricks. The phenomenal skills of the patients were like something from a film with superheroes possessing mutant abilities, but within the asylum there were no special effects or stuntmen. I was about to witness the one amazing superpower that scared me so much that I never wanted to see it with my own eyes, the scary and unstoppable power of super strength. I could not believe my eyes or my ears, but during the early evening of this peaceful night the Whispering Man found his voice. I had always been warned by Mother and many other asylum staff to immediately run and keep running if I ever heard it. I could overpower most of the asylum's patients if I needed to, but not the unbelievable mighty strength of the Whispering Man.

I had been told that this individual could rip fire doors from their hinges with his bare hands like you or I would tear a match from a book of matches. I imagined he could easily squish my skull and all my immature child bones between his index finger and his thumb. I had heard terrifying stories about this patient from many different sources, so I would have definitely placed him on the asylum's top ten list of most terrifying residents. I should have remained constantly fearful of this drugged and psychotic killing machine, but, confusingly, at the same time when calm he would not raise his voice above a whisper and was one of the softest and kindest patients that the asylum had to offer. It was like having a Jekyll and Hyde complex – two opposing personalities.

When agitated, in the gaps between the shouting while the Whispering Man caught his breath, I could hear the raised voices of staff shouting back at him aggressively – which rather than defusing the agitation, only appeared to enrage him further. I became more and more fearful as I listened to the staff denying him his caffeine, which only escalated the situation. I was silently begging them under my breath to surrender the coffee and prevent a major incident.

This was the first time I had ever witnessed this myself, but all the scary tales etched in my mind about the Whispering Man instilled a fear within me that took complete control of my legs and feet as they took off in haste. It sent chills through my body to hear the loud demands for coffee become even louder as they followed me through the asylum, and they were now echoing against the walls of the stairwell and down the stairs behind me. My legs could barely keep up as I ran down the stairs, before disappearing like a gust of wind onto the lower level of the asylum.

As with any animal in the wild where fear is used to keep them alive when surrounded by predators, fear was not a bad thing to hold within you at all times at the asylum as it could keep you alert and thus safe and away from danger. As I ran through the corridors there were several doors that offered me safety from the coffee maniac, but they all led to a secure ward, to a dead end in which I could be followed, trapped and left in even more danger. Anyway, you could not just charge through an asylum gateway and expect protection on the opposite side, as you never knew what, or who, was waiting behind each heavy door. Anticipating trouble with every door you opened in the asylum was wise and kept you safe, and this was one asylum story that I did not want told through another blood splatter on the corridor walls. I did not know what was controlling the Whispering Man that evening, whether it was a superpower, the prescribed medication or the unstoppable desire for the addictive powers of caffeine.

To the untrained eye, he just looked like a caged beast who

had been waiting for the day in which he could release his rage. I was not going to stick around to discover the answer. Now on the lower floor, there were multiple exits available that would take me to the safety of the grounds. The escape route of choice was at the far end of the lower corridor, and with the bellowing demands for coffee becoming louder and louder, I took off running so fast that it must have almost caused a sonic boom. I bounced off the walls of the corridor to steady my sudden acceleration like I was a metal ball-bearing being fired from a pinball machine and pinging off each obstacle in its path. I felt guilty for the patients who I ran past, knowing they were easy prey as they lay in the path of the rampaging psychopath.

I had to remind myself that I could not save everyone from all the perils of the asylum, and that my presence there was only to protect England's secret royal history. My whole body left the floor as I threw myself against the enormous heavy door that stood between me and safety. I had promised Mother never to display the frantic feelings that lay deep in me while I was at the asylum for the simple reason that it would have drawn attention. However, if anybody had seen me acting the way I did that night they would have known instantly that something was afoot. However, that evening the corridors were like a ghost town, bare of any staff, alive with only its helpless and wandering patients. After barging open the heavy door to freedom and safety, I was still not sure where I was headed.

Suddenly I had escaped the confinement of the interior of the asylum and was now spoilt for choice in which direction I could run. I knew that the Whispering Man was much stronger than I was and had the power to remove the door from its frame and, following that, remove all my limbs from my torso, so remaining there and using the door as a protective shield was not an option. I quickly looked left then right, trying to spy somewhere safe to hide. I had to make a quick decision as my life possibly depended on it, but the vast range of evacuation routes left me flustered and confused. In the far distance I could see a large bushy evergreen with huge branches sweeping down to the grassy ground. The unusual shape of the tree made a natural hidden shelter similar to an enormous tepee or an oversized umbrella. I had been there many times before and was aware I could step into this enchanted-looking tree and be completely hidden, as if I had disappeared into a magical wonderland. I headed straight for the safety that Mother Nature had personally placed there for my protection. If I had been an armoured porcupine then I would have rolled off quickly as an indestructible ball, or if I had been a skunk then I would have lifted my tail and sprayed an impenetrable trail behind me. I would have done anything in my power that evening to finally get myself safe and hidden.

I darted off towards the enormous tree. I was running so fast that world records would have been broken that evening if timed; any quicker and my trainers may have caught alight from all the friction.

Thankfully with each step I could hear the volume of the Whispering Man's shouting becoming quieter. However, I did not realise that this meant that the gap between me and another danger was narrowing. Luckily, I thought, I made it to the tree at lightning pace, disappearing into the tall grassy undergrowth that was all around the tree. I was worried that the crunching and rustling of all the branches that I had pushed past to enter the hidden panic room would have alerted any predator chasing me from the asylum to my hiding place, so I remained fully alert with all my senses heightened as I listened for scarily loud and threatening demands, or the smashing of furniture, until I could pinpoint the Whispering Man's location. My silent prayers were answered when the crashing and threats of violence did not follow me, which to my relief meant neither did the Whispering Man.

Once I was completely out of sight and camouflaged, my torso began to unwind and loosen from its petrified state that had seemed to tighten every muscle in my body. Even my breathing began to relax and my heart rate decreased from its frenzied tempo back to its regular pace. I felt so hidden and safe, like the branches of the tree were the warm arms of my protector herself, Mother Nature, who was hugging me and telling me I was now secure under her personal protection. There was nothing in this world that could have moved me from my twigged cocoon of refuge, like a young chick not wanting to fly and leave its nest for the first time. I was about to get comfortable and prepare for a long stay, to stay safe from any continuing violence until I was one hundred percent sure the coast was clear.

That was until the unthinkable happened.

Irrespective of how secure this newly found safe house made me feel, it did not take very long to realise that this private and secluded part of the institution was also used for the most heinous and terrifyingly disgraceful sins of the asylum. I could not believe I had missed it, but right there a little deeper within the bushes was something even worse than that which I had just barely escaped from with my life. I was looking straight at two large men who were struggling with each other. As they became aware of me, they paused from their physical brawl and stared straight at me with their mouths open and an expression on their faces that looked more shocked than a deer caught in headlights. In absolute fear I froze, praying they would just think I was a large branch. I hoped that I was either camouflaged by terror, or that my silence and stillness also gave me the power of invisibility.

Although not at an age when I could fully grasp the

enormity of what was being done by one to the unwilling other, I knew enough to know I was in a bad situation. The shock that I was feeling suddenly turned into trepidation as I watched glistening red blood trickle down from the mouth of the obvious victim and, clearly, the weakest of the two men.

I could not hold my fear in any longer and broke the silence by screaming at both of them, but my screams of terror were only met with equally terrified howls from each of them. I then once again returned the shriek only to be met with an equally pitched holler. If the aggressive attack had not begun again, then this ping-pong match of consecutive harmonic panic could have continued all night.

Sadly, not even my presence could deter the bigger man. As he turned his attention back to the assault, I noticed the victim's leather trouser-belt had been removed during the attack and was left lying on the grass underneath their feet. As I watched, the attacker bent over and picked up the belt and started swinging it hard at the injured party's half-naked body. The dominance of the attacker drove fear into his victim, who barely struggled or put up a fight as his body and arms took the painful slashing of leather. Obviously being non-verbal meant the victim could neither report the attack nor shout for help; all he could manage was the agonised scream that had reflected my own shout of terror.

You could hear a whooshing sound as he swung the leather belt through the air, before striking the metal belt-buckle against his victim's body with a whack. The poor victim had little defence against the now weapon-wielding aggressor, but instead just cowered and screamed, begging with moans for the attacker to stop whipping him. Pinned up against the tree by his assailant, the wounded could not escape the torture and molestation. Instead he desperately pleaded with me, with tortured eyes, to help and not to leave him with the attacker. I could see the trauma and despair in his tearful eyes as he wept. I could see the helplessness in his body as he was barely putting up a fight while his attacker shook and shouted at him to comply with his sexual demands, making him remove his trousers completely. After yet another refusal, the attacker drew back his arm to once again swing and whip the defenceless underdog with the buckle of the leather belt.

Instead of striking the victim's body with a mighty blow, the metal belt-buckle became caught up in an overhead branch. This gave the victim only a short moment of reprieve because after failing to release the belt from the tree and Mother Nature's firm grip, the sexual attack escalated. The assailant pounced at his prey and began ripping his clothes off him. I heard the sound of material tearing as I watched shirt buttons flying through the air.

I shouted at them to stop, but the abuser just turned to face me and swore, then the frightening attack continued. The two unsteady patients fell to the floor, but the assailant remained on top. Held down by the sexual predator, his attacker had partly exposed the victim's genitals and was threatening the victim with more violence if he did not completely expose himself. After hearing these threats and them taking the physical fight to the grassy floor, where they began to roll around on top of each other, kicking up mud and leaves, I became so scared that it pushed me into making the impossible decision to run back to the asylum and my own danger zone – and possibly into the arms of the crazed monster who I had barely escaped so recently. At that decision-making moment, the choice between being part of a physical or sexual attack were equally daunting, but I much preferred my chances against an angry giant over an aggressive, sexual deviant.

Neither of the two options were pleasant or inviting, but when push came to shove a possible fatal attack was more acceptable than any kind of sexual one, and putting my safety aside I needed to summon some help for the poor victim. To be honest, the ruckus was drawing too much attention to the hiding spot so I had no choice but to leave anyway as the moaning, shouting and fighting had made the hideout far too noticeable, like turning the sirens and lights of a fire engine on.

It would have felt pretty awkward if I had stayed because as terrifying as it was, I would have had to shush a rapist to hide from a potential killer, yet another unimaginable scenario that my duties as The Royal Guard had led me to. I was already exhausted from my first escape, and I felt like I was totally drained of all energy and I was ready to collapse. This was only until the time came for me to dodge yet another unspeakable peril that the asylum kept in its catalogue of dangers. As I ran, I could not believe that I was once again headed back towards the asylum and what I had run from moments ago; some people may have said it was a crazy idea, but after what I had just witnessed I preferred the thought of my head being ripped from my shoulders than the thought of my trousers and underwear being ripped from my body. It took everything I had within me to make it back to the asylum.

I was panting and sweat was dripping off my head and through my clothes as I struggled with the gradient of the gradual uphill climb. I was so exhausted that by the time I made it back to the asylum my legs were barely moving forward at any measurable speed. I had to pause for a moment to take some deep breaths and once again gain control over my exaggerated breathing. I stood at the asylum's entrance, terrified to reveal my fate by reopening the door that I had previously escaped from. I was mentally preparing myself to come face to face. This desperate and overpowering desire for caffeine stimulant that could remove doors from their hinges was a far and terrifying cry from the beautiful, calm and sophisticated characters depicted in coffee ads. Instead of false propaganda and marketing that make coffee seem harmless, maybe coffee brands should film their adverts in an asylum, thus revealing its true qualities and mind-altering addictive values.

I put my ear to the wood and listened intensely through the heavy door for the Whispering Man's horrifying screams of terror, but was only met with the regular moans and howls of the asylum. It did not matter how hard I pushed my ear against the door, without hearing the sound of the Whispering Man's voice to act as a signal on my human radar, I felt dead in the water – like a battleship waiting to be torpedoed. He may have just been somewhere in the asylum where I couldn't hear him, or maybe he had been physically taken down by a team of nurses and subdued with psychotic drugs. There was a variety of possible scenarios running through my imagination.

As far as I knew the madman might have just murdered all the staff, having now only been silenced by a mouthful of bloody human flesh. Having been left clueless to the whereabouts of the enormous and enraged giant, I feared the absolute worst, but this was something that I could not shy away from. I had to quickly rustle up all the courage I had to once again push open the heavy door.

I did not mess around and waste any time; once inside again I picked up the pace and began to run down the corridor to find Mother. I accidentally came into contact with a patient as I moved quickly down the corridor, dodging past them all. I think to have made the error I was about to make as I ran, my mind must have been elsewhere – perhaps part of me was still with the man being sexually attacked within the hidden chamber of the tree. The patient that I accidentally struck in my haste began to fall backwards into other vulnerable patients, who I had to quickly grab and prop back up like catching spinning plates falling to the floor from the poles they were spinning on. I had to have the nerves and delicate skills of somebody catching falling priceless vases in a museum during an earthquake in order to prevent the patients cracking their fragile skulls on the hard floor after falling into one another like a toppling row of perfectly stacked dominoes.

Thankfully I was able to save all those falling from the near catastrophe before continuing on my quest. Luckily, I found two members of staff walking through the asylum; my words came stuttering and mumbled from my mouth as I reported the sexual attack as fast as my lips would move. I expected them to act like a rapid response team, sent at any cost, like heroes, to save and rescue the poor soul who was being physically and sexually abused by the other patient. I informed them who the attacker and victim were, then pointed in the direction of their secret and hidden location and what was now a crime scene.

As I recounted what the patients were doing to one another, the two staff members made moans of disgust in distaste and asked me to stop detailing the sordid incident. The lightning movement of them jumping into action was as motionless as a stagnant rain cloud with the timed rapid response of a dead cow. Instead of quickly disappearing with their superhero capes flapping in the wind behind them, the two showed little to no concern for the suffering patient. Rather than dealing with the attack themselves or mounting a rescue party, their instant and only reaction was to laugh, refusing to take my plea for help seriously. To my disappointment they went on to tell me that I should keep safe and stay well clear of the disgusting occurrence. It was as if they spoke on behalf of all the patients at the asylum when one told me quite casually, 'It is just what they do here.' On the flip side of the coin, unlike their attitude to the suffering of the patient in the tree, the staff were clearly concerned about my welfare and safety. The worry could be seen on both of their concerned faces as they pivoted me around on the spot.

They span me like a rag doll on a spinning top, checking my body fully for any injuries. While they did this, I challenged their pleas for silence and continued to explain the attack in detail, to their disgust. After they had seen that I had suffered no injuries, looking horrified, they used the graphic details of my surrendered statement of the experience to teach me, in their eyes, a valuable lesson. Their concern for me intensified and they acted as if I'd just had a near miss and was lucky to be alive. They told me that next time my mother might uncover my naked and lifeless body in a shallow grave if I wasn't more careful around the dangerous patients. I hoped that the staff were just trying to use fear tactics to narrow my boundaries and freedom at the asylum. I think that some members of staff just found the amount of time I spent there with the patients a little bit unusual.

After fear had been drilled into me and everybody had made it crystal clear that they were not going to check on the patient who was being violently molested, I became very worried and even more concerned. As much as I was concerned, at the same time I was too scared to go back by myself to ensure his safety and prevent it escalating further. I walked away sad and utterly disappointed in the two so-called carers and continued on my unsuccessful search for Mother. This all left me with terrible feelings of guilt over not having done anything to save the helpless victim.

The continuous dreadful visions and thoughts of what that vulnerable man was suffering kept flashing through my mind. Instead of discovering Mother and reporting the incident, I had to contain my frantic frustrations after I saw Father poking his cheerful head around the asylum's front door. He had the goat in tow so he didn't want to come in, but I wanted to talk over all the events of the evening with him. However, I knew that he would not take it well if I told him that I was involved in two separate incidents, in which I could have been both killed and sexually abused. I was also far too fearful to tell Father what I had just been through because he would have instantly banned me from the asylum, claiming it was for my own safety. I was also not planning on giving Father the ammunition, satisfaction and pleasure of saying 'I told you so,' to Mother. Instead, Father, myself and the goat walked quietly home. We didn't speak, but the hypnotising clickity clack of the goat's hooves on the concrete pavement made me fall into a trance, lost in deep thought about what I had just witnessed. I was thankful to be alive with my virginity still intact.

It had been pure luck that royalty had not been involved in the uncontrollable violence that took place that evening. Violent episodes were frequent because sometimes a vicious outburst was the only way to be heard within the asylum. The attacks were so unpredictable that they made the institution, and the confined spaces, a place that was far too dangerous to secretly hide members of the Royal Family from the world and the history books. Watching as members of the Royal Family had been left for dead in a place where you had to fight for both food and survival left me annoyed and confused. I spent my childhood looking for answers I could not find. I could never understand how any members of royalty could be forced into this survival mode by their own family when they were already so vulnerable. A place where they would fight for their dignity and life, a place where the severe dangers of this real-life *Hunger Games* ensured that survival mode really did mean survival mode for them.

Now, I saw added dangers everywhere. The grounds were littered with predators of the human variety, from what I was sure had been a paid assassin to sexual fiends who went about their disgusting hunt for victims quite unchecked. Apart from a patient who said she fell pregnant to a member of staff, I was not yet made fully aware of all of the darkest and most sinister dangers that this home to the Royal Family held. Surely the twisted mind of a serial killer or serial rapist would see members of the Royal Family as easy to access, high-level trophies of their sickening acts. I just had to hope the asylum was not home to a Dr Death or any other unsavoury character of that level.

Having members of royalty kept unprotected and vulnerable meant they were possible targets and at risk from planned sexual attacks by not only patients but also members of staff. This was something even The Royal Guard could not protect them from – yet. It was as if the Royal cousins' lives were being played with like the pieces on a chessboard, or they were contestants in a barbaric sport such as fox hunting, with them as the prey, and rather than giving them a quick and painless death, you watch them physically and mentally suffer for as long as possible in a multitude of unthinkable ways. It terrified me to think that people like that, with those capabilities and lack of empathy, were the architects of the world that we all live in. Having royalty in this dangerous place meant not only their lives and souls were at constant risk, but their bodies were also.

I myself could have been raped and murdered in just a single evening at the asylum, so you can only imagine the pain and suffering that the members of the Royal Family had been forced to endure during the decades they had spent there. Maybe it was part of the cover-up and giant masquerade to consequently ensure the words and actions of people around members of royalty at the asylum did not meet the standards that any other able member of the Royal Family would ever expect or accept. Rape was accepted in this home of the Royal Family, either because it was so frequent that it became unmanageable or because people really just put that little value on these individuals' lives.

I could not imagine for one moment that any able member of the Royal Family would live somewhere they would have to accept that being raped or molested was always a possibility and just part of the package of their surroundings. I could not imagine any of them being made to feel that worthless and unloved as a human being while having nobody watching over them and keeping them safe. With the press giving us stories of lives of luxury that the Royals live and still complain about even then, I was getting increasingly angry at the injustice. I spent my time at the asylum in a state of hypervigilance, with rapists on one side, rampaging mental patients on the other, and the added threat of a possible attempt to wipe out the evidence – the assassin I was sure I had spotted.

It makes you understand a little more why their voice boxes may have been removed to silence these royal mouths and maintain the secrecy, even within the asylum. As they were already dead to the world, and no funds were contributed to their welfare as members of the Royal Family, I was unsure why anyone needed to end their lives for a second, more deadly time. They were forced to live without any form of royal security, so anyone set on killing them would have no real obstacle – or so the royals thought. They had no idea that their discarded family had me, The Royal Guard.

The asylum had been a place where I saw physical crimes against royalty taking place on a regular basis, crimes for which people in the world beyond the asylum would spend their lives in prison for committing. The value of a human being within the walls of an asylum was very different to its worth on the outside; even a priceless royal life was without value here. This changed when the royals in the asylum won their champion. I spent most of my childhood trying to insert myself between the royals and those who would harm them.

Little did I know that the letter I had written to the head of the family, to the head of the state, was going to make their lives far more dangerous. There was never going to be an official Rolls Royce rolling down the drive at the asylum to whisk these poor members of the family off to one of the many palaces and castles the family inhabited. When I was very young I used to think that none of this made sense. Surely it would have been kinder and safer to have the Royal Family's secrets chained up in dungeons or locked away in the Tower of London, instead of hiding them in an asylum with all the dangers and perils that a prison for the unwanted holds? Absolutely anything was possible at this asylum and it was the one place in England where the unthinkable really did happen, the place where the dead could still breathe and have a pulse.

Through it all, I still held out hope that the new generation of royals would come to the rescue. I imagined these poor family members were a secret to them, as were the sins of the previous generation. I was so wrong.

Chapter 16
The Safe House

It seems to take a greater amount of courage to be kind than it does to be cruel. The harsh elements and cruel conditions of this world were not made by the heat from the sun or the rain from the clouds. It isn't the wind or the snow. What I saw as the cruellest and life-threatening conditions creating unforgiving environments were that of human words and contact.

I wasn't just taught, I was shown at a young age from the highest level what a cruel and unforgiving world we live in. A world in which the weak, elderly and vulnerable are regularly preyed upon. I witnessed humans lay a path of more pain and suffering than any unforgiving storm could bring, destroying lives and changing history. Like a tornado ripping through your lives and leaving devastation behind so that nothing is ever the same again. Leaving you dead to the world. Tearing homes from you and all your clothes, belongings and fortune. Like being picked up by a tornado and then dropped where nobody knows you or your name, and all the family you once knew were gone. Wealth stolen, banished, and you are accepted as dead. They had no ruby slippers that could transport them to where they truly belonged when they clicked their heals; neither was there a yellow brick road to follow and get them back home safely.

It marks you when as a child you question your whole society, as I did. When you wonder, should we not have leaders who lead by example instead of leaders without compassion for even the vulnerable individuals of our world? Should our institutions, especially the monarch, not have evolved from our most barbaric times in history? Should our monarch not be a positive example, and not allow people to remain labelled and prejudged because of their abilities or by how they look. Followers of such leadership are led by example down a dark and slippery slope headed towards abuses such as neglect, bullying, hate crimes and racism. These bring anxiety, depression, self-harm and even suicide for the innocent victims.

The Royal Family were just as cruel and no better than the children I saw playing in the streets, who teased and called the patients unkind names. I could do nothing but raise my voice at them to stop. I could shout at some of them, but sometimes I could do nothing but stand idle and watch as patients ran in fear when empty cans or bottles were thrown at them. Maybe it was the asylum's messy dress code, the badly-fitting clothes, which made people turn up their noses, and I guess that having to call the Asylum for Idiots 'home' did not help strengthen their case for equality within the local community. Without ever being made to truly feel part of it, some patients lived among this community, in homes that were very close to the asylum.

It seemed strange to see some of these individuals return to the institution, but the desperate need to feel accepted and included was so strong that it drove these individuals back to that unpleasant and evil place. They craved to join regular conversations between people without a disability, rather than the limited vocabulary and groans of the other patients. These individuals who returned to the asylum were more equipped to endure all the perils that the institution had to offer. It seemed that less abuse was suffered and the dangers of the asylum were limited if you had your mobility and a voice.

Some of the staff did not appreciate the extra patients hanging around the asylum, but Mother convinced these lost souls to find her each night that she worked. They were encouraged to remain under her protection not only with friendship and deep conversations but also by the regular flow of tea, coffee and biscuits. It was inspirational to see them so happy. I sat there with them on the ward drinking cups of tea as I watched in awe of Mother. It would get me thinking about the different world that we could live in, a world filled with love and kindness instead of hate and envy. To me, Mother was a glowing example of how things could be so different with an alternative perspective. Unlike anywhere else I had seen, when in the presence of Mother these individuals felt like they had formed a real friendship.

However, as I got older and became more aware of the world, with the memory of that figure at the fireworks display, I sometimes succumbed to suspicion on these poor souls who had nowhere else to go to find human contact. I often sat there and looked at the happy faces and imagined which ones were real and which one was a cunning disguise, hiding a cold-blooded royal killer. The problem was, I could never decide on one. Every time I was at one of Mother's sessions I would fluctuate between possible culprits. Was it that scar that made me prejudiced against one guy? Were that woman's crossed eyes why I didn't trust her? Was I as bad as those can-throwing hooligans on the street?

Through these and similar experiences I learnt from a very

young age that our body has an internal reward system, which is so complex and precise that it could have only been given to us by our creator. Do good things and good things truly do happen, and the rewards all begin from within our fully functioning internal mechanisms, which most people ignore through their own ignorance. We all have an internal moral compass that, if listened to, not only keeps us on the right path, but also commands internal rewards of fulfilment, joy and purpose within our own bodies that money can't buy. Like a drug, a simple act of kindness can fill your whole body with a natural high, leaving you on cloud nine. I should know. In contrast, there are moments when something can fill you with fear and loathing all at once. This happened to me one winter night as I left the asylum after one of Mother's sessions with those patients who lived in the community. It was cold and dark, and a light snow was starting to fall as I pulled on my thick gloves and woolly hat before I got on my bike. In the winter, I didn't walk the grounds in the dark. Not even the self-appointed Royal Guard had that much courage. My mind was on getting home and into the warmth, and I was thinking about the homework I still had to finish, when I felt a hand on my shoulder and sensed that whatever was standing behind me was big – very, very big.

'Your mother is an amazing woman,' a voice that sounded like it had been bombarded by several packs of cigarettes a day for decades wheezed into my ear. I could feel the warmth of the man's breath as he crouched down to whisper. 'So brave to let all those mental patients have such easy access to her. You never know when one of them might turn violent. I hope she stays safe.'

'Why shouldn't she be?' I whined, my heart almost stopped from fear, my blood colder than the falling snow.

'Oh you know, people sometimes misguidedly take up a

cause, take on responsibility for others who they should avoid, and good people end up getting burned.'

I was really shivering now, but not from the cold. Terror had overtaken all my senses, as I realised that my mother might pay for my self-appointed role as the royal guard. Frightened as I was, I was determined not to show it and tried to turn around to get a look at the enemy, but he was too close and had somehow penned me in between his body and the wall against which I had my bicycle balanced.

'Hello, can I help you?' came the voice of a woman, and in that instant the man took a step back and I turned to see Lucy, the defender of the oppressed and nemesis of Leanne, standing there in a bright-red, fake fur coat and a black woollen hat pulled down to just above her eyes. She was wearing some very high heels, which I imagined would fit very nicely between the man's eyes if he tried anything.

The man turned and I could see he thought about moving towards her for a second, but there was something in her eye that made him decide against it.

'Just saying hello,' he gasped and turned quickly on his heels and marched away like a very heavy duty soldier.

'Are you OK?' Lucy asked.

'Yes, I'm fine don't worry,' I said, still a bit agitated.

'You can always talk to me, you know that, little one,' Lucy said with a look of real concern in her eyes. 'You are not alone, I promise.' With that, she also turned and walked away into the night.

What did she mean, I thought, standing there unable to move and really confused about what had happened. Was she one of us? A Royal Guard? Was she there to protect the Royal cousins? Who put her there, if she was? The Royal Family? 'Unlikely,' I whispered and watched my breath leave my mouth in the white cloud of a winter's night. I was in a mystery even deeper than I had imagined, that much I knew.

If Lucy was one of the good guys, then who was the man? Was he there to make sure the Royal cousins were never discovered? Had he just threatened to kill my mother if I carried out my duty? Which of these two were sent by the royals? Was it this strong and brave woman, sent to protect them, or the scary guy, sent to harm anyone who would dare to protect them?

As I stood trying to work out what had just happened, the asylum siren started to shriek and mayhem ensued. People ran in and out of the asylum, and all of us outside were told to go home quickly.

'What happened?' I asked one of the nurses from the night shift, whom I had known for years.

'Tinky is missing and there is a lot of blood on her bed,' he shouted. 'Get as far away from here as you can.

My heart leapt out of my chest. Had I been distracted by a double act while the assassin had crept in and done away with the royal cousins?

All hell broke loose and people were running here, there and everywhere calling out for Tinky. I guessed that it was one thing to cover up the Royal Family's crimes against their own family and quite another to lose the evidence of that dreadful crime.

I was standing by a clump of trees just outside the asylum door when I heard a gentle 'pssst'. I turned round to see Lucy hiding in the dark of the trees.

'Tinky is missing,' I said, just in case she hadn't heard all the shouting.

'I know, we hid her from him,' she whispered.

'Him? Who?' I spluttered.

'No matter, she is safe in the big greenhouse just next to

the entrance to the tunnels. Now, go and find her and become a hero.'

I didn't wait to ask any more questions but dumped my bicycle and ran as fast as I could through the snow, the ground under my feet so slippery that I fell several times. I knew she would be terrified, and I was afraid she would wander off in the dark and do herself some harm.

I got to the greenhouse to find Tinky huddled in a corner whimpering like a lost animal. It broke my heart. However, the smile she gave me as I took her arm and helped her up off the floor made up for all the nastiness of the night.

As we made it back to the asylum's main door I saw Mother standing talking to the head of the asylum, a balding, paunch doctor who had not set foot in any of the wards for as long as I could remember.

'We have to call in the police,' I heard Mother say.

'We can't,' the paunchy one replied. 'You know what the ramifications could be to all of us.'

As Mother looked away in exasperation she spotted me and Tinky. 'Oh, thank God!' she shouted, and then some thought clouded her eyes. 'Did you take her?' she asked me.

'No, Mother, of course not. I just had an idea about where I would hide if I was in the grounds in the dark and cold, and there she was.'

Strangely, no one asked me where that was as Doctor Paunchy tore the Royal cousin out of the arm I had put round her and almost dragged her back into the asylum, Mother running behind them mumbling, 'Be careful, don't hurt her.'

The incident was never mentioned again, but that evening I learnt three things: I was not alone as The Royal Guard, bad people were after the Royal cousins and meant to do them harm, and most upsetting of all to me, Mother was part of the cover-up – or at least she knew more than she was letting on.

We have all felt the system at work inside us, the internal system that gives us a sense of happiness relayed as a warm or good feeling when we do something kind or giving. The system has been made so user-friendly, it even tells us when we are on the wrong path with a rotten feeling internally preceding an unkind or bad act. Similar to a farmer gathering his crops from a field after long preparation and months of strenuous labour, it may not be easy to master and to stay on course, but with hard work the rewards are great.

After that night, my system felt like it was definitely in good order and I had finally been part of something important. However, I would have preferred to have handed over the Royal cousin to a warm and loving family and not back into a cold and sterile asylum.

The system is even set up so that these internal positive feelings are so fulfilling that they lead to further kind acts in chase of that feeling once again, and I certainly wanted more of that high. I was no longer prepared to sit and watch, I wanted to serve and protect, as the New York police department puts it.

Maybe Mother was also chasing these feelings, despite what she had to turn a blind eye to. She always went above and beyond what was expected of her, or what others were prepared to do. With busy roads, rivers and accessible railway tracks all local to us, Mother would not settle if she thought that wandering patients were not safe. While other houses in our neighbourhood had elaborate home alarm systems with loud sirens and flashing lights to keep their families safe, we had a security goat. It was just our regular goat placed at the front of the house. Unlike other alarm systems, our goat was not linked up to the local police station for an immediate dispatch of a trained squadron; instead the goat alerted us to intruders by loudly bleating at anybody walking on the street by our home. Consequently, our house was not found by wandering patients completely by chance.

Father seemed to enjoy regularly blaming my goat ownership for our house being discovered and the consequent random knocks on the front door by patients, but really it was him who decided we had to move the goat from the back to the front garden regularly due to my goat destroying our grass with its hooves on a constant basis. My father insisted we had to rotate where he grazed to preserve the lawn.

It seemed that even the most able and toughest of patients was scared of my goat or any other of our family pets. Our family home was like Noah's ark and you would often see patients running and screaming in fear from our house. We possessed turtles, cats, a dog, hamsters, rabbits, a tortoise, doves, stick insects, just to name a few, and that is not including the multitude of wild animals that we fed – such as foxes and deer. I guess some would say that my family home was similar to the asylum, a place where predators and prey are forced to live together in harmony because of their need for food, comfort and shelter.

While Mother enjoyed tea and cake with our visitors, I would gather up a variety of pets and surprises to parade before our guests. One at a time I would show them all of the animals that I could find. My house was a new world that they were alien to, and depending on the patients' nerves and level of fear, I could sometimes only display my chosen pet through the window or just a narrow crack in the door. I was much more enthusiastic about the whole animal-sharing experience than the patients, but that did not defuse my excitement to entertain them.

However wary the patients were of our pets, they enjoyed visiting our home so much that they eventually learnt to get along with them. Over time, barriers were broken and fears were lifted. When the weather was good, we were even able to have refreshments in the garden in the company of my goat. Often when my father was at work and not around, Mother turned our house into an asylum while breaking her own rule of not having patients in our home. She would regularly invite round some of the other staff to join her and the tea-guzzling patients, and I would always be happy to see the larger audience attendance for my animal shows. One day I sneaked into my parent's bedroom on a mission to retrieve clothes so that I could dress up and put on a performance for the visitors from the asylum. I marched down the stairs and presented my outfit to everyone sitting on the sofa and armchairs in the lounge to everyone's astonishment and delight I appeared as a ringmaster dressed in my father's long, sweeping and oversized tailcoat jacket.

From the side table, I picked up and tightly rolled Mother's magazine to make myself a loud microphone, then I eagerly placed my lips against my freshly assembled megaphone and released a bellowing announcement that immediately stopped all other conversations and raised people's heads from what they were doing. Then, for their enjoyment and entertainment, I transformed our home and garden into an extravagant circus along with exotic performing animals.

The show began when I entered the arena by riding on the back of my smartly dressed goat, who wore my father's rather gaudy Hawaiian shirt and a purple tie. My lion-taming act was wooing the audience and going brilliantly, until the dog released an uncontrollable 'woof' instead of a ferocious roar. I think it was that bark that gave it away, though I don't believe I was fooling anybody disguising the dog as a lion by using a ball of my mum's orange knitting wool loosely wrapped around his head to represent a hairy mane. To make my performance even more realistic I made a lion tamer's whip from excess wool tied to a long piece of garden cane. Mother shouted at me abruptly, telling me that I wasn't allowed to whip the dog even with the soft wool, even if he had ruined that part of the show by barking instead of roaring.

I was just about to object when I saw one of the visitors who was standing away from the rest, by the garden gate. As my eyes fell upon him, he made a gesture, raising his fingers to his eyes and then pointing them towards me, in the universal signal for 'I'm watching you'. If I had a real lion I would have set it on the man, who I recognised as the one who had threatened me the night Tinky went missing. I opened my mouth to shout a warning to Mother, but the man had already turned and disappeared out of the garden gate. I was angry, but I was also a little afraid. Why couldn't they leave us alone? We had protected their secret for years. Then I remembered my letter to the Queen. Could she be behind this intimidation? Could it be the Duke? I was confused and frustrated. I had had such dreams of the monarch's Household Cavalry riding to the rescue.

A little fazed, I knew I had to go on and decided to introduce my personal favourite performer on the day, Speedy the tortoise. No one could tell how hard my heart was pumping from fury and terror as I had Speedy jumping through hula hoops and running assault courses made from plant pots and garden furniture at record time. Speedy had the potential to be the spectacular death-defying highlight of the show, but to my disappointment Mother refused to make it as realistic as possible to an authentic circus by dousing the hula hoop with petrol and igniting it so that my tortoise could leap through the ring of fire to the deafening roars of the cheering spectators.

Looking back, it is strange to think I was one of the only

people in the world who held the deepest, darkest of royal secrets, but at the same time I was a happy and innocent child putting on shows with dressed-up pets for the entertainment of the hidden souls who had been confined to the asylum.

Sharing these new and extravagant experiences with the outpatients was rewarding, and their honest, excessive and uncontrollable appreciation made my body tingle with a warm sensation inside, which replaced the fear and anger. I could only imagine that the feeling is similar to that of the first time you watch your child riding a bike independently, without stabilisers. It felt amazing sharing these moments that meant so much to them; laughing and smiling with them meant the world to me and I soon let go of the image of the man and any sinister intent he might have.

It was not only about these energetic and high-energy moments; we also shared quieter and more peaceful moments when we had time to talk deeply, which would give me time to reflect upon all our lives. We attended the morbid and somewhat less dramatic church services together with the outpatients each Sunday morning, and at other times they would accompany me on a dog or goat walk. I realised that these individuals had not experienced life like I had. Our lives were worlds apart and I imagine that spending time in our home with my family felt very different to their regular existence.

I always enjoyed taking any opportunity to quiz anyone who knew the secret about their amazing royal memories from the asylum, and the perfect moment to do this seemed to be during the times when they would join me to walk my goat through the asylum's grounds. They were fully aware that the goat played a much greater role in society and was not there just for petting and our entertainment, as he was probably the first goat ever in history to play an important part in the lives of the British Royal Family. My goat never chose the gangster life he had; the gangster-goat life chose him. I had made him a part of the secret royal conspiracy – if I was the hero, the goat was my sidekick. I am sure that without that goat I would have never stumbled upon what I did at the asylum. Perhaps while protecting the world's royal history that goat actually prevented yet another royal scandal, or just maybe all those royal patrols accompanied by the goat around the asylum's grounds were actually the beginning of the end for those sacred royal secrets.

Chapter 17
Spies and Non-Existent Lies

I admit it, we were probably not the world's most likely or obvious crime fighting duo, but we were brought together by both the secret and unusual circumstances of these hidden and breathing dead members of the Royal Family. Since the goat had been banned by Mother from entering the asylum, we were left policing just the exterior together. Admittedly, my goat much preferred patrolling the outside, as he spent a large portion of the patrol munching on the fresh lawns as if the asylum's grass were a rare delicacy that could not be found elsewhere. Daytimes and evenings, whatever the weather, we always kept our heads in the game and our eyes peeled for any suspicious, or out of the ordinary, movements. I never had a clue as to what I may come up against, and after hearing all the throat-slashing stories I lived in a state of constant fear, especially when I was forced to protect the world's secret history by patrolling the inside of the asylum alone and without my horned and hoofed sidekick as back-up.

There was that one time when my goat nearly chased a

member of the Royal Family to her death, but apart from that one minor hiccup the goat was an asset to the team. I had seen animals being sponsored and raising huge amounts of money for charity, and I had even seen police dogs pulling children from burning buildings, but my goat deserves a place in history and should have been knighted for his contribution to society and protection of the royal conspiracy that would eventually shake the world. My goat was having more input in the secret royals' lives than their true family for the simple reason that the goat did not prejudge or hold prejudices against disabled people.

Looking for any unusual behaviour during my royal patrols of the asylum, I would follow any new faces or suspicious characters. One day while pulling the goat behind me through the cut grass on the stunning front lawn of the asylum, I glanced towards the main building and noticed a pair of eyes staring straight back at me. Leaning against the wall in the distance was a gentleman whom I had not had the pleasure of meeting before. I kept glancing back at him and noticed that the pair of eyes was following me as I walked around the grounds with my goat. It was not unusual for people to stop me on my walks to say hello and pet the goat, so I put his interest down to him noticing the unusual sight of a boy walking a goat around an asylum. He looked nothing like the thug that had previously threatened me. This guy was quite delicate and appeared to be in the uniform of the asylum's cleaners. His face looked friendly and safe to my child's eyes.

Due to the slowness of the ambling goat, my observer had disappeared by the time I had returned to the main building after circulating the front lawn. A few weeks later I noticed the same man emptying rubbish into the large external bins. I could not see it at first but as I wandered closer I noticed him with what seemed to be a small camera. He was so involved in what he was doing that he didn't notice me at first, but as soon as he heard my goat's hooves trotting in his direction, he immediately hid the camera. As we got closer, he looked at us both with an awkward smile on his face. His grin left me feeling uncomfortable and I released an equally awkward chuckle before I asked him if he wanted my goat to pose for a photograph, in an attempt to break the obvious icy awkwardness between us. No words left his lips; he ignored the question and instead just roared aloud in a fit of laughter as if he had never heard anything so daft in his life.

The behaviour did seem weird and a little suspicious, but I didn't have any sense of what it could mean. As one of the cleaners, he was somebody I would get to meet and talk to again now that the initial contact had been made, however awkward it had been for us both. I began to notice him more and more around the asylum; we would pass each other in the corridors and acknowledge one another with a simple nod of our heads. One day I caught him in mid-conversation with another of the cleaners, and I was intrigued beyond belief by him. This was the first time I had heard any words pass his lips. I was surprised and struggled to listen as I could barely hear any of the mumbling chatter.

I noticed that although the other man looked worried and stressed, he also had to keep bending to get closer in order to understand what the first cleaner was saying. I could not hear what he said, but it was clear that he was talking in pidgin English with such a deep and husky voice. Something within those broken sentences instantly raised my suspicions. I was not sure whether he had a very strong Italian or maybe Russian accent – it definitely was not English. Had I stumbled upon a foreign spy? Maybe this would lead to me uncovering yet another evil royal plot, possibly one to permanently silence their dishonourable secrets. This was the depth of excitement that I had been searching for, and this kind of small but significant detail was all that a boy who grew up watching James Bond movies with his father needed to launch a more thorough investigation.

Once I heard his accent my imagination ran wild, and I was left to dwell on a list of possible outcomes – if he was just posing as a cleaner and it was a cover for something else. I imagined that perhaps it had been decided that these immoral secrets and lies that could seriously harm the Royal Family had to be silenced once and for all; with agents in place it would only take a simple phone call or wink of the eye to give the order. There could end up being a pile of dead bodies in order to completely clear up their royal conspiracy's web of lies, and being a cleaner would be the perfect disguise for anyone sent to do the job. At any moment, I could be snatched and thrown in the back of a van and taken to an unknown fate, perhaps killed, all to protect these dark secrets of heartlessness, lies created to cover up any hint of weakness in the royal bloodline. Sometimes, late at night, I would sit in the dark in my room and imagine what it would be like if they took me and threw a bag over my head, leaving me in darkness.

I speculated how they would take me to somewhere very remote and torture the secrets from me. Certainly, my family's and my own welfare could be threatened as I would be put under immense psychological pressure, or for all I knew my poor mother may open a parcel one morning to find my fingers or other parts of my anatomy.

Already officially dead, I was concerned that if the Royal cousins were just taken elsewhere to 'disappear' again nobody would go looking for them. How do you even report a dead person missing? It would certainly take quite a lot of explaining to the police. I imagine that if you came up with a story about the walking-dead members of the Royal Family, you would end up locked in an asylum like this one before anybody would believe and take you seriously.

Whatever the risk, I had a mission and so I launched my investigation into this stranger by questioning other staff, but nobody I spoke to knew anything about him. Most of them didn't even know he existed, which worried me even more. For the moment his true identity remained safe as he seemed to possess the mindset and skills of a ninja, working in the shadows and keeping himself to himself.

To battle the obvious counter-surveillance skills that he possessed, I set up lookout posts whenever I was at the asylum. He manoeuvred like a chameleon, adapting to each situation so as not to stand out. I observed him walk silently from place to place as if he were tiptoeing to keep under the radar. The more intensely I watched him, the more I started to believe his job as a cleaner was just a cover for something much more sinister. The possibilities were endless; it was unclear whether the reason why he was at the asylum was for me and the royal secrets. He may have been sent to kidnap the royal cousins and hold them for ransom, or even to use the sinister royal secrets to blackmail the government and Great Britain. If the accent was Russian then he could be a Russian spy sent on a secret mission to assassinate the British Royal Family with a poison or toxic gas.

If the strong accent was from Italy then maybe it was one of the Italian mafia wanting to torture us and trade the secrets or demand a ransom from the British monarchy. I was making no quick or irrational judgements because I had not heard any reports from around the asylum of horse's heads being found in any of the royals' beds, or any other signs of the extreme measures that a mafia family would inflict to send a clear warning to the British Royal Family.

I hid around corners or looked inconspicuous inside the wards to gather my own evidence. As I spied on him, I noticed that he did not really do much cleaning for somebody who was hired as a cleaner; he mostly pushed his broom around the floor without purpose or emptied bins of trash into rubbish bags. I remained on the cleaner's trail, but I did not find it easy to uncover any more hard evidence. One day when I was at the asylum I had an eerie feeling and glanced over my shoulder to catch the cleaner watching me. Thereafter, it seemed that each time I looked over my shoulder he was there. I think he was spying on me just as much as I was running surveillance on him. We began to closely watch each other, waiting for one another to make the first mistake. We were playing a game of cat and mouse.

One very early Saturday morning, I was abruptly shaken from my deep slumber by Mother. I could barely open my eyelids but as I rubbed my eyes clear of any gunk, I could see an enormous smile and pure excitement lighting up her face. She had returned from a night shift at the asylum with a piece of folded up paper. She briefly unfolded the paper and flashed it in front of my face to reveal indecipherable pencil scribbles, before immediately folding it back up. Excited, I snatched it from her hand, and once again unfolded it to look more closely at the scribbles. My eyes were instantly drawn to a symbol of a crown in the centre of a configuration of other shapes and contours of all different sizes. Then mother snatched the paper from my hand, turned and walked far enough away that the paper was now out of my reach and protected from my grasp. As she left the room, she screeched back at me from out on the upstairs landing, saying in her most excited voice, 'Quickly get up, dressed and ready for an adventure.'

I immediately arose from under my snuggly duvet and shot out of bed, throwing on the clothes slumped over the end of my bed, which Mother must have chosen for me to wear before she woke me. I got dressed and my feet barely touched the ground as I ran downstairs to properly greet Mother in the kitchen. I could see that she remained lit up with excitement like a Christmas tree. I could not stand the build-up of suspense as she refused to give anything away about what was ahead. I gobbled down the cereal she put in front of me as I sat at the table in the lounge, filled with anticipation of the promised exciting day ahead. My spoon was in motion like a machine and my throat was constantly swallowing like a conveyor belt set at maximum capacity. I was throwing my breakfast down myself in haste, similar to that of the royals as they ate their food at the asylum, always in fear of someone taking it from them.

Between enormous mouthfuls of cereal, the cornflakes exploding and flying across the room each time that I spoke, like an attack from an automatic machine gun, I repeatedly questioned Mother on what the crown symbol meant and pleaded to be told what all the other shapes on the piece of paper that she showed me were. Annoyingly, and to my great disappointment, Mother wished to keep the suspense going, acting like the piece of paper was a priceless sacred manuscript. She did well to hold her excitement in. I could see that she was struggling not to burst out with the grand climax of our forthcoming adventure, spilling the beans and revealing the momentous mystery. Instead, the smile that was all over Mother's face was telling me that she was enjoying being extra cryptic, and she continued adding to the confusion of the enigma by telling me that we were going somewhere that doesn't exist to see something that also doesn't exist. As we closed the front door of our house, Mother told me to grab the goat as we would need him as cover. I untethered him from the post and the three of us walked down the driveway and, to my surprise, headed out in the opposite direction to the asylum. The confusion was heightened as I had definitely seen a royal crown symbol scribbled on the paper.

We ambled along at the goat's pace for about ten minutes before she reached into her pocket and pulled out the folded piece of paper containing the handwritten, coded drawing. She unfolded it just as we arrived at our destination and the place where the explosive details and the importance of the upmost secrecy were all going to be explained. She turned to look at me with a serious expression on her face, then told me that she was going to give me my final lesson and complete my education in royal conspiracy.

She explained how this was a top secret mission and we could not be spotted by anyone. I could tell by both the excited and concerned look on her face that this was going to be far from the usual clean, fun family entertainment provided by regular parents from a normal household. She had just raised the gauntlet of excitement to a whole new level. She had to place her hands on my shoulders to stop me jumping around with excitement. 'Calm down, darling, we are about to enter a cemetery so you have to be calm and respectful.' I nodded my agreement. 'Oh, and keep the goat off all the graves and definitely don't allow him to eat any of the beautiful flowers left by people's loved ones.'

'I've got it, Mother. Now tell me what we are doing here,' I demanded.

'You'll see soon enough,' she said with a broad smile on her face. She put a hand on my back and quickly but calmly directed me through an iron gate and into the graveyard. I was happy to see there was no restriction on the entry of goats onto that hallowed ground.

The cemetery was full of people, however they were all dead. We seemed to have the whole cemetery, above ground, to ourselves. The ghostly quietness was excellent news because I found it difficult to look inconspicuous around people when accompanied by a goat. Mother reached into her pocket and retrieved the piece of paper. As she unfolded it, she explained that it was a secret royal map. She pointed to the symbol of the crown as our final destination. She continued to tell me that today we were going to be searching for the member of the Royal Family who had died twice. I was trying to understand everything while my goat was pulling on the rope and attempting to steal the flowers on the graves for his breakfast. The goat was drooling over the beautiful bouquets of freshly cut flowers; I had to tug hard on the rope to keep him from munching on any. I think he would have eaten every single flower petal in the entire cemetery if I had released my grip from his tether.

It was a huge cemetery with thousands of graves; without the map we would have never stood a chance of finding what we were looking for. Drawn in the centre of our map was a square shape, which looked to be in a similar place to where the cemetery's chapel was situated. It seemed like a good marker, so we headed straight for it. As we wandered down the paths past all the graves to get to the chapel, the spookiness of the cemetery and ghostly atmosphere was broken by signs of life in every direction. There were enormous trees with huge canopies of green, red and yellow leaves, which brought such vibrant life to a place filled with horror and death. The added peacefulness and tranquillity made you feel like you were standing in the Garden of Eden. You would never have believed that such dark and minacious royal secrets were hidden here. After reaching the chapel, we headed off down the path in the direction that the royal map sent us.

We were nearing the crown symbol that was marked on the map, meaning we were closing in fast on our secret destination. As we walked closer, Mother once again highlighted the importance of us not being spotted, and I began to feel nervous, as if we were criminals participating in a major heist. As we neared where the crown was marked, there was an eerie sense of royal history in the air. We began to sweep down the rows of graves; it felt awkward because we had to walk over many of them to see the names printed on the tombstones.

It did not matter how many times we flipped it around, turned it upside down or just checked the map regularly, the crown symbol on it was telling us that we were definitely in the correct area, so we just persisted. We remained unable to find what we were looking for, so we just kept scanning the site and reading each and every name chiselled on the tombstones. It seemed as if the map had taken us as far as it was going to; we were now on our own using just our eyesight to desperately search. In frustration, I handed the rope with the attached goat to Mother so that I could take the lead in the search and speed up the process. I pushed the search forward but struggled to read all the graves because many of the headstones had weathered, victims of the harsh elements over time. The goat had a better perspective on some of the graves than I had, so I kneeled down on the grass so that I was on the same level to him. I then read the names on the long-forgotten graves, ones that were cracked, smashed and knocked flat onto the grass. If anybody had seen me they would have thought that I was just a small child imitating a goat in a cemetery, not a Royal Guard on a top-secret royal mission.

I had no luck with any of the tombstones that lay flat, so I jumped up on my feet and continued searching down the rows of graves. I ran my fingers over the uneven surfaces of the chiselled out names as I walked down each row reading every headstone. All of a sudden my fingers stopped moving across a small white T-shape cross; instead they froze on the individual, cheap, and probably tiniest cross in the cemetery. With a pure rush of adrenaline and excitement tingling through my body I shouted over to Mother, 'I've found it.'

She shouted back at me to shut my big fat mouth and stop shouting. Mother pulled on the rope that was wrapped around her hand and dragged the goat straight over to me. She was as desperate as I was to see with her own eyes the astonishing secret royal grave that didn't exist. Mother and I read her surname and the unusual serial number. Little did she know, but our family now shared the same blood as the royal below our feet. She was my blood-sister's sister.

Without saying a word to each other we took a moment to bow our heads and take it all in, showing respect with our silent words. This was a very, very difficult pill to swallow. I was extremely surprised that the ground beneath my feet was not rumbling and shaking from her turning in her grave. It felt like I should be crying and more upset than I was, but instead of tears it was intense anger that I felt around my face and cheeks as I gritted my teeth. Inside I could feel the shame of what they had done to her; this was just before I felt the tragedy turning into rage as it began lighting a fire within my belly. The grave was disguised as the resting place of an unimportant nobody, camouflaged by the other surrounding unimportant and forgotten graves. The grave was without a tombstone, family crest, flowers, cards or any sign of love, making the solitary emptiness of this top-secret location feel eerie.

We had to keep checking over our shoulders and all around for anybody watching us at that historic site, but luckily we seemed to remain completely alone. I could not believe that I was staring at yet another secret part of our history books, and yet another part of this royal conspiracy. This was a royal who had died twice, and it really brought to the surface yet another ill-fitting piece of the puzzle. Imagining her lying there under the soil in a pauper's grave, stripped of everything royal in death just as she was in life, was both a shocking and a disgusting sight. The Queen Mother's niece may as well have been strung up and nailed to a crucifix as a spectacle to show the world what your fate would be if you ever dared to be born disabled.

'This is her, the one who died at the asylum?' I asked Mother, wanting it not to be true.

'This is her, darling.'

'Why alone and discarded?' I said in anger, making my voice quake.

'They couldn't bury her twice, could they?'

'But they did, first in the asylum and then in this dump,' I shouted.

'Shssssh, control yourself, the trees have ears.'

'I don't care, I want to make them pay.'

'I know, darling, I know. We all do, but we might end up next to this forgotten royal if we make this public.'

My body shook with the pain of what had been done and how unfair it was, and the frustration that if I spoke out I could risk the lives of everyone I loved. I wouldn't put it past them to cut the goat's throat as well.

This kind of punishment was a lesson in life that would only be taught in the Pontius Pilate school of hard knocks; it was a sentence to a piece of sacred history that would be solely applauded by him. Maybe this spectacle that I was staring at was a threat or a warning to all the other members of the Royal Family, that disabilities will not be accepted and will be punished severely. Mother kept having to silence me with a 'shush', but I had so many questions that needed answers. After seeing the horrid and unkept grave, such a contrast to the beautiful cemetery, I had to suppress the negative feelings that overwhelmed me. If I had known then that this cemetery would end up having even more royal paupers' graves marked by small and simple wooden crosses like you would have in your garden if you had buried a dead rabbit, then I'm not sure that I could have kept my emotions under control.

I turned to face Mother and told her, 'I wish that I could raise her from the dead and lay her where she truly belongs.'

'Maybe you will one day. Maybe you will grow up big and strong to fight all the evil in this world,' she replied with a smile.

Those powerful words from Mother resonated and remained with me. Mother put her arm around me to comfort me and show solidarity. I think this was the moment that Mother understood the depth of my emotions and feelings for the lost and forever forgotten Royal cousins. I realised that the grave before me stood for everything that is wrong in the world. A burial and headstone that she truly deserved for this deleted piece of the world's royal history was the least that should have been done. She was born different but she was still part of our history, to be passed down from generation to generation and never to be forgotten. This was a sight that you would truly have never believed really existed except in the movies. This secret grave showed me the extreme lengths of the corruption within the Royal Family. This was a corruption of life, wealth, leadership, history and our humanity.

The feeling that consumed me on that day has only grown over time, and through royal tragedies, but it has never faltered.

I wanted to return to the grave with flowers but Mother would not allow it, saying it was too dangerous to do that or even tell anybody that we were ever there. I immediately defied her and picked some daisies from the ground at the graveside, then placed them on the Royal cousin's grave before we left. This new secret meant that I was now a part of a royal conspiracy within yet another conspiracy. As we walked back home with the goat, Mother made me promise that I would never return to the grave. At the time I agreed not to, but that was a promise I could not keep forever. Instead, I would visit the grave often, but covertly and without my parents' knowledge, as the cemetery and the secret royal grave were only a few minutes' cycle ride from my house.

It was an important day in my life, but once back at the asylum I continued my regular patrols and kept my promise to Mother to not tell a soul about our secret mission to the royal grave. I kept one eye out for unusual activities, and when I could I kept the other watchful eye on the suspicious cleaner. I continued trying to listen to his conversations in case I could overhear anything incriminating but found his accent too strong to make head or tail of his ramblings.

One day I blew my cover when the cleaner caught me standing watching him, mesmerised by the brushstrokes of his broom. He could see my obvious interest in him and calmly strolled over to share a few words with me. Before I knew what was happening we were standing next to one another, and he was muttering something that I did not catch, so I had to lean in and ask him to repeat himself three times. I was the guard, the spy, but I found myself being interrogated about my mother and my goat. He mixed up these questions with casual enquiries about school and hobbies to gain my trust and lure me into a false sense of security. I believe it was at this moment that he began grooming me. After hearing his voice over and over again, as he had to repeat himself each time we spoke, I gathered that it was an Italian accent that I had been struggling to understand, but I was never one hundred percent sure. I struggled to translate the English words that he knew, making the language barrier between us an obstacle, but the cleaner continued to persist with the friendship and sought me out whenever I was at the asylum. It felt as if this unusual new friendship had an ulterior motive and was definitely leading somewhere.

One day after having shared idle chitchat on many occasions, he approached me, obviously looking around the corridor to ensure that we were alone and without witnesses, which made me feel very uneasy all at once. He looked all around to double check one last time that we were both alone. This was the moment that his fake friendship and continuous grooming had been leading up to. In one fell swoop, and out of view of any witnesses, he tried to take both my honour and my dignity. He grinned as he put his face closer to mine and placed his hand on the back of my head, before pulling my face towards his. I was frightened and tried to awkwardly pull away from his tight grasp of my head when I saw his lips move closer towards me, but they just kept coming until they reached my face and then it happened. I gasped before I felt his warm breath on my skin as he whispered into my ear in broken English, 'You know royal here?' I was flabbergasted. I could not believe it. I tried to hide the instantaneous shock and stunned look on my face as my jaw dropped to the floor in horror at what he just asked me. It felt like my entire body's warning system had just been alerted and placed on defence mode with a pending imminent impact.

It was obvious that this had been crossing his mind for some time. Similar to a volcano, he had worked himself up until he reached his magnitude and the day came when he felt comfortable enough to erupt and speak to me about the royal secrets that were imprisoned at the asylum.

I answered him with 'Royal?' as I shrugged my shoulders with a puzzled look on my face in my most theatrical manner. I acted like he had asked me the surname of somebody who I did not know. This also gave me time to think ahead about my answers to what was obviously coming, a royal interrogation.

'Royal Family,' he quietly replied, still in a whisper. I had clearly heard what he had said but I still leant in and made him repeat the question, as I could tell by the murmurs in his voice that he was nervous about both the private interview and, more importantly, saying the word royal aloud. I tried to look confused by the question. I knew it was not my place to tell anybody about the royal secrets that the asylum kept, and as their official guard I was going to keep their secret as closely as anyone – until I could free them properly. I stood back, releasing myself from his grasp. I looked directly at him with a look on my face like he had just said the moon was made of cheese. I shook my head vigorously and told him that I knew nothing about any royalty at the asylum.

Although I made it crystal clear to him that I had no knowledge on the subject, he persisted with the questions. I shook my head every time. Then he reached into his trouser pocket, pulling from it a crisp five pound note. He told me that I could keep the five pound note if I got him any information from the asylum about the Royal Family. I silently chuckled to myself because facing me, on the front of the banknote that he was holding up, was a portrait of the Queen. Had he taken the trouble to look, he would have realised that the picture resembled and had all the characteristics of one of the secret Royal cousins whom he was in search of at the asylum. Talking with me about the Royal Family was the mistake that I had been waiting for. He had made a huge error by trying to bribe the wrong person with the wrong question. Apart from that, I felt he was bidding far too low, as the precious information I had on the Royal Family was worth a great deal more than five pounds. I was not in a position to start haggling over the price of my royal secrets because I was not going to sell out my Royal Family and blood-sister. This unusual request made me super suspicious of the cleaner, even more than I was previously.

I continued to act dumb and divulged no information. Remaining silent on the subject was what Mother had drilled into me over and over. The cleaner eventually gave up asking me and continued to go about his business, but the offer remained on the table. I waited until he was out of sight before I dashed through the corridors and found Mother – who to my surprise was with Tinky in her office. I had to catch my breath before I could get my words out, but when I eventually could, I told her what had just taken place and the possible threat to the asylum's royals.

Mother knew of my concerns about the cleaner. We now spoke about the royals quite openly when we were alone. Two defenders working together to guard a secret and to work to free our royals one day.

As soon as I blurted out news of the cash offer she finally took me seriously. Then everything changed, as I had imagined that Mother held the secret just as I did, as an outsider. However, the moment she heard about the incident with the cleaner she quickly, and stealth-like, unofficially put the Royal Family on red alert, requiring an instant reaction to the threat.

'Darling, I fear they are not safe here anymore,' Mother said as she took charge of what I thought of as Operation Royal Guard. We were now, both of us, officially the royal guards, pledged to ensure the safety of those discarded members of the Royal Family.

The royals were placed on lockdown, hidden from view.

Tinky and one of the other royals whom mother got to quickly were immediately shoved into one of the less accessible back bedrooms. We had two of them safe and locked down. Then I followed mother as she made her way along the corridors, and I felt the breeze on my face from the ward door as she slammed it shut. You could hear the increased pace of her footsteps as she ran into the office to hide any files that had royal names on, so that their true identities were covered up and no longer visible and on show.

When we were sure we had done all we could to protect them, Mother placed her hands on my shoulders and sat me down in a chair. She looked at me straight in the eyes and once again repeated the strict instructions, if ever questioned again to lie and deny all knowledge of everything royal. These are not the usual requests of any mother, but my family were forced to live the life we did and had to protect the royal secrets at any cost. While other children were being taught the difference between right and wrong, I was taught to lie to protect the Queen of England's lies.

Without drawing too much attention, Mother began to quickly spread the word among her colleagues. Not only was the cleaner being watched carefully by other staff, word had spread and a careful eye was also placed on all of the royals. Without alerting the cleaner to the investigation, Mother began to gossip. People did not believe my Russian spy or Italian mafia scenarios; they were more inclined to believe that it was just somebody with an unhealthy personal interest. Mother told me that he may possibly be a reporter, but he did not seem intelligent enough or even fluent in our language.

'We can't afford to alert him to the fact that we know who he is,' Mother told me, so I just carried on as normal, passing him in the corridors day after day and just nodding and smiling. He would smile and say hello as he did before, yet now each time his greeting would be followed by a short and awkward laugh as if he knew he'd made a huge mistake by blowing his cover to question me. He did not know that it was already too late, but he clearly did not want me announcing what had happened so tried to remain on friendly terms with me. He went as far as asking about the welfare of my goat, clueless to the idea that the goat participated in many royal patrols.

It seemed like the goat and I had a hidden identity to protect, like Batman and Robin. We did not have to keep our capes hidden for long because it was not too much longer after the incident that the cleaner disappeared and we never saw him again at the asylum. For all I knew his disappearance could have been because the goat and I had started a chain of events that led to a hit being taken out on the cleaner himself. Maybe this is what happens when you become too close or knowledgeable about this royal conspiracy; maybe my own disappearance was already in the making and I would be the next one to unexpectedly vanish.

If throats could be slashed and voice boxes removed to prevent these royal secrets spreading like the coronavirus, then I could not put anything past the Royal Family's willingness to destroy the lives of others, no matter how vulnerable they were. Possibly putting the royals on lockdown while denying any access to them did the trick and had the desired effect, but without the use of a wig, dark glasses and a fake plastic nose, I imagined it was pretty impossible to hide my royal blood-sister, who resembled the crowned lady whose portrait was on each and every circulating banknote, coin and stamp in Great Britain.

Maybe all those royal security patrols with the goat had actually prevented the royals from being kidnapped or even assassinated. The goat and I possibly saved the secret lost history of England from being lost all over again, and I am sure that losing it once more would have probably meant it would never be found. What I do know is that these huge royal secrets that could shake the world and turn the secret Royal Family's lives upside down, will not remain a secret forever.

Chapter 18
The Warning

There was now yet another secret that I held, which the rest of the world did not. As I walked those spooky asylum corridors at night running my fingers across the brickwork with the gentleness of Romeo running his fingers through his lover Juliet's hair, those stories told in bloodstains on the walls rushed through my body, which now held my very own secret royal tale. I felt it with every ounce of my being. I was in a real-life fairy tale mixed with horror. I was in a fairy-horror tale! The whole world knows that some princes are born surrounded by wealth and extravagance at Buckingham Palace, or with chefs and champagne and teams of over twenty medical staff on Lindo Wing, but what the world did not know was that other princes are made in the blood- and faeces-stained corridors of a dark, dirty and sinister asylum.

There may have not been an easel outside Buckingham Palace to announce it, but like a phoenix rising from the ashes of the conspiracy, I had tapped into the Queen of England's bloodline and the asylum now had its very own little prince, handcrafted with royal lies and regal deceit. Some may say my imagination and reality were blurring into one and that I could no longer see what was real and what was not. This was not the case, as for a child my imagination was not that wild. I could not imagine or make up a life this crazy; it was my reality that was delusional. What I did know was that there is something about being the blood brother to a dead member of the Royal Family, hidden and abandoned, that just changes you. I felt the royal blood flowing through my veins. Those sinister and dark corridors had made their very own little prince out of me.

The Royal Guard, Prince of Madness had a lovely sound to it each time I walked the corridors saying it in my head or out loud when I could see I was completely alone, still fearing that I would let the secrets out. Being the only blood relative to give love, affection and attention, it was killing me not being able to tell anyone. Some days it felt like I was going to explode with all the secrets I was keeping. I know that I went above and beyond my duties as The Royal Guard, but what better way to protect royalty than with a bond and promise now made in blood?

I know we all like a happy ending, but all the signs were crystal clear and right there for anyone to see. I honestly believe that I'm a prince, but we all know differently, don't we, because I cannot be the only one who can see it. Like Godzilla and King Kong, a hero or a villain needs time to emerge, but you can see the monster that the Royal Family are creating and what is beginning to happen when a child's belief system is destroyed and his idols become his rivals.

The asylum was a part of me and within that asylum, where I was surrounded by royal figures, I was becoming part of the 'rabbit hole' while being taught lessons through real life that no classroom would ever have taught me. To me it was simple; they just had to do the right thing with our sacred history instead of leaving those royal individuals to be unintentionally found by me, having been thrown out like trash, forgotten and left to rot by our noble and honourable history keepers. I watched as they paid homage and spent millions on preserving historic royal buildings but not a penny on preserving historic people. Any system is broken when you have enough funds to fix everything yet choose to ignore and only add to the neglect and suffering. This goes beyond the years of pocket money that the Royal Family owes me for buying regal clothes and treats for their family members.

My childhood scribbles addressing these problems in the form of a letter addressed to the Queen at Buckingham Palace was still in the post, or possibly headed somewhere much, much worse. The nation and even the world are growing tired of the lies; it feels like the Royal Family are losing touch with their people. How can you show loyalty to your countrymen when you show none towards your own family? The Royal Family worried too much about what they unjustifiably felt was the shame that the disabled members of their family could bring upon them, that they weren't paying attention to what else a dishonourable royal conspiracy could produce – a monster who could bring equal shame upon the royal household.

During my short life this far, I had not witnessed a single day where abuse and suffering were not forced upon the royals at the asylum by the able members of the Royal Family. It was the lies and maltreatment against their own that gave birth to me, the royal guard.

It was shortly after the failed assassination attempt that I began to wonder who else they were hiding. Were there more disabled individuals, homosexuals, lesbians, misfits, substance abusers or rebels? I guess it could be anyone whose elegance had escaped them or just those who did not make the cut.

Maybe I will act like a lighthouse, a beacon, or maybe people will see me as the Batlight that shines brightly over London as a reassuring sign while calling out to other abandoned or hidden royal rejects to show themselves by coming out of the shadows, because they too are treasures who have nothing to be ashamed of anymore. Whatever the reason, I had become the royal guard for all those who had been discarded by this dysfunctional family.

If their voice boxes remain intact, then I imagine the ones who can talk may have already been silenced, like puppets, with money and a lifestyle way beyond their dreams and means that they are afraid to lose. I often wondered if there were others like me that God had created to counteract the royals' actions and to bring some balance to this cruel and unfair world. The yin to their yang, the chalk to their cheese, the light to their darkness, the good to their evil. Soon I started to believe that I was created to be the Royal Family's nemesis, even though I was never looking for justice; instead I just wanted the royal cousins to be safe instead of spending my life picking up the pieces of the family's barbaric crimes against humanity.

If I ever met the royals I would tell them, 'Even though you portray yourselves as them, you are not gods. All you are is a dysfunctional family like the rest of us, but actually you are nothing like the rest of us as you are much more dysfunctional, as proven when you lawlessly killed your own and banished them from your kingdom into a life of torture, pain and suffering.' Maybe I could teach the Royal Family something they are missing; you might be surprised what you can pick up from a humble kid from the gutter who has been asylum born and bred. Maybe from my own experience they could gather some tips on ruling a mighty kingdom, a royal household and a dysfunctional family. I bet that most of the world didn't even know that Great Britain had two fully functioning royal families? Each was just functioning very differently than the other.

While one was a money-making business performing, dressing and acting as if they were in a pantomime, the other was in survival mode, in fear of what was behind every closed door while each day and night was spent fighting for its life. Also on the advice front, I'm not one to shy away and be afraid to give dangerous answers to even more dangerous questions that have never been asked. I am only limited by the simple fact that I can only tell you the truth and nothing more.

After that first terrifying day at the asylum when Mother threw a fearful little boy to the pack of wolves who were hungry for human contact, I did not imagine that I would come back as the alpha, gaining their trust and one day leading the asylum's wolf pack, who indirectly helped to bring me up. It may not have happened yet because for now the wolf in me is hidden under sheep's clothing, but it will. A lifetime of protecting the history books will do that to somebody and put him on a rocky path chosen with his heart, one that he will not falter from. I will always protect my wolf pack and do whatever it takes to survive the cruel world within that asylum. Maybe it was OK when they were just messing with their own Royal Family, but when they abandoned them and together we were forced to share a family, that was the moment they messed with the wrong Royal Family. My Royal Family. I am reminded of all the sacrifices and the bond I share with royalty each and every time I see my royal blood-sister's reflection in the face of the Queen on each and every banknote I touch.

They ignite something inside me like putting gas to a flame or more heat to a screaming pressure cooker; they make the blue blood that flows through my veins boil when I see the able-bodied members of the monarchy for who they truly are, ferocious and sinister bullies. They are just big bad wolves. To them I am nothing, just a harmless little piggy in a tiny and feeble straw house, compared to the mighty brickwork of castles and the fearless armies that they hide behind. Well the Royal Family can huff and they can puff, and each and every one of them can individually 'blow me'.

I already knew back then all that I know now, but just in much less colourful language. Fuck the system. Fuck your broken system. Fuck any system that destroys lives.

I was going to play it safe, just keeping my head above water like a shark fin, but maybe I'm here to make the monarchy feel uncomfortable and pay them back for all those years of sleepless nights and royal nightmares that they put upon an innocent child. Maybe, just maybe, they should be a little bit scared about the monster they have created with their torture, abuse, lies and royal conspiracy within those asylum walls, because this is just my chorus and I have already changed history and drawn first blood. My mother calls me an angel while my father calls me a devil, but you can call me The Royal Guard.

Printed in Poland
by Amazon Fulfillment
Poland Sp. z o.o., Wrocław

24798355R00133